# THE SPIRITUAL
## HEALTH OF THE
# WARFIGHTER

A Biblical Model for the Professional Warrior

CHAPLAIN KORY M. CAPPS

From the Fray Publishing
8103 Stonefield Way
Tampa, FL 33635

www.fromthefray.com

# TABLE OF CONTENTS

INTRODUCTION

# A Blueprint of a Godly Warrior

"Chaplain, is it okay to celebrate when we take out our enemies?" Questions about faith hit different in a military setting. My friend threw this one out on a four-month deployment in the Middle East. For the next couple days, we hammered through this question as we looked at different passages of Scripture, read articles, and listened carefully to differing views on the issue. For those few days, we labored at the intersection of faith and the military profession.

The complexity of the question became apparent as we read contrasting texts of Scripture: "Do not rejoice when your enemy falls, and let not your heart be glad when he stumbles" (Prov 24:17) and "when it goes

5

well with the righteous, the city rejoices, and when the wicked perish there are shouts of gladness" (Prov 11:10). We recognized a similar tension in Christianity Today's article on Osama Bin-Laden's death, which surveyed diverse Christian responses to that historical moment.[1] Categories began to form in our minds: rejoicing in justice is encouraged, gloating over enemies is condemned, anything that robs a human of God-given dignity is wrong, loving an enemy is complicated for a vocational warrior, and mental wellness is reflected in how warriors deal with enemies.

This was no philosophical exercise; my friend was assessing his current posture and calibrating his future response to the next mission when casualties were inflicted. The gravity of our discussion landed on me and reinforced the importance of grasping how faith informs the profession of arms. The following pages move in the same vein as that deployment conversation and work toward the same critical end; to develop warfighter theology for men and women like my friend

---

1 "How Should Christian's Respond to Osama Bin-Laden's Death?" Sarah Pulliam Bailey, https://www.christianitytoday.com/news/2011/may/how-should-christians-respond-to-osama-bin-ladens-death.html.

that will assist them in navigating the grave ethical and spiritual complexities of wearing the uniform.

The biblical model proposed here centers on the life of David, the epitome of a warrior who exercises faith. In fact, the narratives of David are filled with warfighter theology. It is difficult to find material in 1-2 Samuel, 1 Chronicles, and Psalms detached from the theme of war. Specifically, these narratives provide access to the interior life of a man of God (1 Sam 13:14) and a man of war (1 Sam 16:18).[2] In David, godliness and vocational

---

2 "For David there is one verse that contains a remarkable concentration of descriptive terms. The qualities in this verse furnish a useful structure for examining David's early life. They also summarize the traits he exemplifies throughout 1 Samuel 16-1 Kings 2." McKenzie explores the six descriptive terms: 1) skillful in playing—music played an important role in the temple worship...it was also used to induce prophetic trances...and to keep away or exorcise demons and evil spirits. David was known as the sweet psalmist of Israel (2 Sam 23:1), the author and organizer of the Psalms. 2) a man of valor—some translate as 'nobleman,' the literal meaning of this Hebrew expression is a 'powerful man'...it is a reference to social standing. 3) a man of war—this item refers to someone with considerable experience and success on the battlefield. His skill as a warrior was the single most important attribute in his rise to power...David's skill as a warrior is a key ingredient in the Bible's description and probably in the career of the historical person as well. 4) prudent in speech—Literally it means 'clever of word.' It indicates David's familiarity with proper protocol among the upper class. It also suggests his shrewdness and intelligence

warfighting intersect.[3] This convergence provides a practical model for those in the profession of arms.

1-2 Samuel reveals a man consistently exposed to combat.[4] And "there was war again" (1 Sam 19:8; 2 Sam 21:15, 18, 19) aptly summarizes the context of the stories of David. As a warrior, he was highly respected by his people and celebrated for his valor (1 Sam 18:7, 16). He was held in high esteem by his brothers in arms for his prowess, discipline, leadership, humility, and faith (2 Sam 17:8, 10; 23:13-17). This esteem and

as well as his facility with words. 5) a man of good presence—may point to his handsome appearance or a general good presence. 6) the LORD is with him—God's favor, presence and support of David throughout his life, warfighting and ruling. Steven L. McKenzie, *King David: A Biography* (Oxford: University Press, 2000), 50-66. See also, Steven L. Mckenzie, "Who Was King David?" *Word & World* 23, no. 4 (2003).

3 Walter Brueggemann suggests that the narratives of David are woven together with ethical and practical fabric. "The interface of tensive complexity in the text and tensive complexity in life suggests that in communities of faithful interpretation, such texts as those concerning David are not to be read, understood, and interpreted, but also practiced as a way of attentive life, a life of fidelity." Walter Brueggemann, *David's Truth: In Israel's Imagination and Memory* (Minneapolis: Fortress Press, 2002), xvi.

4 1 Sam 17, 18:7, 19:8, 21:9, 22:20-23, 25:28, 28:1-4, 30:1-31; 2 Sam 3:1, 5:19-25, 8:1-6, 10:4-18, 18:7, 21:15-19, 23:8-39.

respect given by his battle companions and community extended to his enemies (1 Sam 18:30, 29:4-5).[5]

David was well experienced in his vocation. He led small units of warriors, commanded elite troops, had charge of hundreds and thousands of soldiers, and eventually was the chief over an entire army (1 Sam 18:3, 22:2, 23:1-5; 2 Sam 12:29, 23:8-39). He knew life on the front-lines and experienced calling the shots from the back (1 Sam 17; 2 Sam 21:17). He was a combat-proven veteran and leader.

David's combat exposure was profound. Called a "man of blood" (2 Sam 16:6-8), his temple-building aspirations were denied because of his scarlet-stained hands: "You have shed much blood and have waged great wars. You shall not build a house to my name, because you have shed so much blood before me on the earth" (1 Chron 22:8).[6] He took many lives, saw many

---

5 Avigdo Shinan states that the predominant character that emerges of David is "that of a tough warrior, a man of reckoning and a shrewd statesman." Avigdo Shinan, "King David of the Sages," *Nordisk Judaistik* 24, no. 1 (2003): 54.

6 Donald Murray links Yahweh's refusal of David's temple building to the purity laws in Numbers. He states, "in Numbers killing in battle is treated, uniquely in the Hebrew Bible, as ritually defiling, making the defiled a danger to the community until they have been decontaminated

lives taken, and lost friends, family, and loved ones. David's combat experience spanned roughly fifty-five years.[7] The narratives in Samuel, Chronicles, and Kings,

(31:19-24)...David's wars were divinely ordered and blessed, since in Num 31 such a divinely ordered (31:1-7) and blessed (31:8-12) battle results precisely in religious contamination (3:19-24)." Apparently, the sheer amount of blood shed by David's hand disqualified him from the temple project. Donald M. Murray, "Under YHWH's Veto: David as Shedder of Blood in Chronicles," *Biblica* 82, no. 4 (2001): 469, 475. Pierce holds a different position; he argues that bloodshed excludes David from building the temple because warfighting is not God's ideal. "If David's excessive participation in war is what disqualifies him from building the temple, then shedding blood is not the ideal, and thus God does indeed operate within a different ethical framework than humans." Madison N. Pierce, "War: Fighting the Enemies of God, not Man," *Biblical Theology Bulletin* 43, no. 2 (2013): 82.

7   David was 40 years old when he became king (2 Sam 5:4). David reigned as Israel's king for 40 years (1 Kings 2:22). He was anointed to be king and fought Goliath as a young man (1 Sam 17:33). Leslie McFall, "The Chronology of Saul and David," *Journal of the Evangelical Theological Society* 53, no. 3 (2010), 524-528. David's pastoral vocation was a significant primer for becoming a warrior. Kenneth Bailey, *The Good Shepherd: A Thousand Year Journey from Psalm 23 to the New Testament* (Downers Grove: IVP Academic, 2014), 40, 50. The Middle Eastern shepherd faced regular danger and harsh physical elements that consistently tested his physical, mental and spiritual strength. The rod was the traditional weapon of the shepherd, and proficient use of the rod was essential for survival and protecting the livestock. David's skill with this weapon was demonstrated against formidable animals; this experience equipped him for battle (1 Sam 17:34-35). Christopher Skinner, "'The Good Shepherd Lays Down His Life for the

as well as the Psalms of David, are not shy about the impact of the profession of arms on his soul.[8]

David was not just a man of war; he was a man of God. He was a worshipper of God, a man of prayer, and a lover of God's word. The only thing more pervasive than combat throughout the stories of David is faith. David was a "man after God's heart," a warfighter with an interior life aligned with God.[9] How did his faith

---

Sheep' (John 10:11, 15, 17): Questioning the Limits of the Johanine Metaphor," *The Catholic Biblical Quarterly* 80 (2018): 102. Skinner notes that Middle Eastern shepherds were particularly vulnerable to two common external threats: "thieves and wild animals...it was not uncommon for wandering individuals or even marauding groups to attempt theft of sheep in such isolated locales." David's shepherd years were an important training ground for his warfighting vocation. Mental toughness, physical strength, weaponry skills, facing down threats, and working through fear were certainly all present in his shepherding experience.

8 Jan Grimell, "Contemporary Insights from Biblical Combat Veterans through the Lenses of Moral Injury and Post-Traumatic Stress Disorder," *Journal of Pastoral Care & Counseling* 72:4 (2018), 244-246.

9 There is debate regarding the Hebrew text of 1 Samuel 13:14. The traditional view argues that it speaks to the interior quality of David. For example, "it is a key thematic interest in the narrative of 1 Samuel that Yhwh's chosen agents have a right heart, and it appears that there is something about David's heart that makes him an ideal candidate to function as Yhwh's chosen one." The other view suggests that the point of the text points to the "royal substitute's like-mindedness to

inform his vocation? How did his view of God impact his view of war? How did his spirituality influence his leadership? Did his walk with God impact how he viewed his enemies? How did his faith inform his painful and conflicted combat experiences? How did he stay spiritually healthy in the midst of so much bloodshed?

These are critical questions for understanding the

---

God, which stands in contrast to Saul's tendency toward disobedience: 'Yhwh has sought for himself a man [whose heart/will is] like/in accord with his [Yhwh's] heart/will.'" In both cases, the heart of David is aligned with the heart of God. Jason S. DeRouchie, "The Heart of YHWH and His Chosen One in 1 Samuel 13:14," *Bulletin for Biblical Research* 24, no. 4 (2014): 468, 484. According to George Athas, Acts 13:22 quotes this text and confirms that the description of David coincides with one who does the will of God: "And when he had removed him, he raised up David to be their king, of whom he testified and said, 'I have found in David the son of Jesse a man after my heart, who will do all my will.'" George Athas, "'A Man after God's Own Heart': David and the Rhetoric of Election to Kingship," *Journal for the Evangelical Study of the Old Testament* 2, no. 2 (2013). For Amos Frisch, David, the doer of God's will, becomes the paradigm and standard for all following kings. Amos Frisch, "Comparison with David as a Means of Evaluating Character in the Book of Kings," *The Journal of Hebrew Scriptures* 11, no. 4 (2011), 19-20; Greg Goswell, "King and Cultus: The Image of David in the Book of Kings," *Journal for the Evangelical Study of the Old Testament* 5, no. 2 (2017): 167, 186-187.

intersection of faith, spirituality, and the warfighting vocation. In the following pages, eight themes in David that live in this intersection will be explored: 1) the warrior's posture towards God's Word; 2) the warrior's relationship with God; 3) the warrior's view of war; 4) the warrior's view of the enemy; 5) the warrior's connection to community; 6) the warrior's mechanism for processing combat; 7) the warrior's sin, shame, and guilt; and 8) the warrior's gospel dependence.

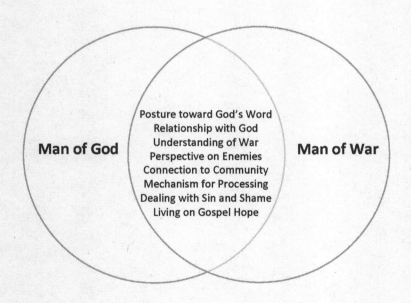

# 1

# The Warrior and
# the Word of God

David was a man of God's Word. The verbs used
to describe his relationship to the Torah reveal
his devotion: love, delight, seek, listen, meditate, long
for, learn, keep, store up, rejoice at, cling, observe, seek,
sing about, hope in, teach, do not stray from, stand in
awe, remember, and praise.[10] The divine summation of
David's life affirmed his passion for the Word of God (2
Chron 6:16). In contrast to Saul, David embodied the
expectation that the Warrior-King of Israel would read
the law "all the days of his life, that he may learn to fear
the LORD his God by keeping all the words of this law

---

10 Psalm 16:7, 17:4-5, 18:21-22, 27:11, 19:7-11, 25:4-5, 33:4-6,
40:8, 56:4,10, 119:1-176.

and these statutes, and doing them" (Deut 17:19; 1 Sam 15:1).

The Psalms are filled with expressions of David's commitment to God's Word. As the preeminent psalmist, David is credited with authoring around half of the 150 Psalms.[11] Many scholars also affirm the Davidic architecture and ordering of the entire book.[12]

---

11 James H. Fraser, "The Authenticity of the Psalm Titles," a paper presented for the degree of Master of theology, Grace Theological Seminary, 1984, 87-88; Jerome L. Skinner, "The Historical Superscriptions of Davidic Psalms: An Exegetical, Intertextual, and Methodological Analysis" (PhD diss., Andrews University, 2016). According to James Mays, "David appears in the psalter in three important ways: in the ascription of some psalms to settings in his story, in the simple attribution of many psalms to David, and in what is said about David in the text of a few psalms." James Luther Mays, "The David of the Psalms," Interpretation 40 (1986): 151. Contra this position, see Tod Linafelt, Timothy Beal, and Claudia V. Camp, The Fate of King David: The Past and Present of a Biblical Icon (Edinburgh: T&T Clark, 2010), 153-154.

12 "That the Psalms were the prayer book of David is a very ancient exegetical opinion." Gary A. Anderson, "King David and the Psalms of Imprecation," Pro Ecclesia 15, no. 3 (2006): 271. Tremper Longman affirms Davidic authorship of the majority of the Psalms. He also argues that David played a key role in structuring the book of Psalms. Tremper Longman III, How to Read the Psalms (Downers Grove: InterVarsity Press, 1988), 38-39. Daly-Denton argues for Davidic authorship based upon the New Testament's unquestioning affirmation of this reality. Margaret Daly-Denton, "David the Psalmist, Inspired Prophet: Jewish

This is an essential point for warfighter theology. Why? Read through a certain lens, the Psalms are a warfighter's handbook. Many, if not most, psalms were written by a warrior in the context of war.[13] In the stories of David, he seems to be holding either a sword or a lyre, waging war or writing psalms (1 Sam 19:8-9).

The warrior has much to glean from the Psalms, not

Antecedents of a New Testament Datum," Australian Biblical Review 52 (2004): 198. Kaiser shows the centrality of David in the structure of the Psalms. Walter C. Kaiser Jr., "The Structure of the Book of Psalms," Bibliotheca Sacra 174 (2017): 3-12. See also, Norman Whybray, Reading the Psalms as a Book (Sheffield: Sheffield Academic Press, 1996) 22;

13 Mays, "David of the Psalms," 145. "The songs that came out of his life as shepherd and warrior, as refugee and ruler, were the inspired expression of a life devoted to God in bad times and good, and therefore the guiding language for all who undertook lives of devotion…Music had a role and function in relation to the needs and important occasions of social life. Its four primary settings in early Israel seem to have been social celebration, warfare, incantation, and cultic rituals." Vivian Johnson explores Psalm 18 as a standard example of a thanksgiving song to Yahweh "for military success." Vivian L. Johnson, David in Distress: His Portrait through the Historical Psalms (Edinburgh: T&T Clark, 2009), 112. Whybray suggests that scholars read the Psalter through three grids: 1) spiritual guide or handbook; 2) public recitation by the community; 3) manual of instruction. Whybray, Reading the Psalms as a Book, 31-32. Arguing for psalms as a warfighter guide/manual would lean heavily on 1 and 3 while including elements of 2.

least, the fact that the godly warrior lives by and operates from the Word of God. Many scholars have noted the programmatic function of Psalms 1, 19, and 119.[14] These psalms provide a "hermeneutical lens" through which to read the entire book.[15] Of note, these three psalms all have the Word of God as their main theme. If the psalms are a warfighting manual, then the Word of God forms the center of soul training for the warrior.

---

14 "They were not psalms in the strict sense but were intended to constitute a framework to the whole body of psalms, giving it the character of a manual of piety based on the central concept of the Law." Whybray, Reading the Psalms as a Book, 18. According to Nancy Jeung-Yeoul Bang states, "Psalms 19 and 119 form a 'macro-torah frame' to support the whole Psalter where I call both 'torah pillars'…the centers of the first and last Books of the Psalter—seems very intentional in that they encourage readers to read the whole Psalter through the lens of the torah motif." Jeung-Yeoul Bang, "The Canonical Function of Psalms 19 and 119 as Macro-Torah Frame," The Korean Journal of Old Testament Studies 66 (2017): 279. See also, Nancy L. DeClaisse-Walford, The Shape and Shaping of the Book of Psalms: The Current State of Scholarship (Atlanta: SBL Press, 2014), 1-85; Kent Aaron Reynolds, Torah as Teacher: The Exemplary Torah Student in Psalm 119 (Boston: Brill, 2010), 140-183.

15 Psalm 1 provides the readers "with 'hermeneutical spectacles' through which to view the Psalter as a whole and meditate on it, seeking for themselves the will of God as expressed in the Torah…it points forward to the Psalter as the medium through which Israel now responds to that word." Whybray, Reading the Psalms as a Book, 21. See also, Kaiser Jr., "Structure of the Book of Psalms," 6.

In David, the reader sees a warrior grounded in God's Word. His practice of interior discipline included meditating, studying, memorizing, and applying Scripture. He drew hope, perspective, joy, and life from his study. He opened himself to the convicting, reproving, and correcting function of Scripture. He allowed God's Word to shape his moral code, inform his leadership, and drive his warfighting.[16]

David's legendary moral failure with a deployed spouse and a faithful troop inverted his positive relationship to God's Word. When the time came for kings to go to war, David remained at home (2 Sam 11:1), thus situating the Bathsheba/Uriah narrative as a war story. By remaining home, David was susceptible to the sinful attraction of another man's wife. He pursued the vulnerable Bathsheba, who was the wife of one of his most faithful warriors Uriah (2 Sam 23:39), and had sexual intercourse with her. In so doing, he betrayed his God, violated a warrior's bride, decimated his conscience, robbed a brother in arms, and killed a loyal soldier: in sum, he "despised the word of the Lord" (2 Sam 12:9). Straying from God's Word has dire consequences for all, the warfighter included.

---

16 Psalm 1, 19, and 119 bear out these affirmations. David's intimate knowledge of God's law would have included Mosaic warfighting guidance, pre- and post-war rituals, godly warrior models, and other essential reading for the warfighting vocation.

In short, the holy text is foundational to warrior health. The warrior must be more than a warrior; he must be a scholar. Steady footing comes from consistent study, attuning one's moral compass requires regular meditation, protecting the conscience demands careful application of scriptural principles, navigating combat challenges and pitfalls necessitates walking by the light of God's Word. The spiritual health of the warfighter is grounded in the Word of God.

# 2

# The Warrior's Relationship with God

As a warrior, David's walk with God was his lifeline. This fact is woven through the fabric of the stories of David. At every turn, he is found seeking God (2 Sam 24:25), trusting (1 Sam 17:46-47), praying (1 Sam 23:2), praising (2 Sam 6:14), glorifying (2 Sam 22:1-51), lamenting (2 Sam 1:17-23), seeking forgiveness (2 Sam 12:13) and relying on God (1 Sam 30:6). In 1-2 Samuel, there are 567 references to the God of Israel, which speaks to the pervasive presence of the divine in David's story (1 Sam 16-2 Sam 24). In truth, David's biography is the story of his relationship to God.

His theology was robust, boasting a high view

of God. As the architect of the Psalms, he exhausts metaphor to describe God: king, sun, shield, refuge, shelter, portion, tower, helper, rock, strength, redeemer, shepherd, light, salvation, holy one, habitation, defense, righteousness, joy, highest one, shade, keeper, song, mercy, warrior, praise, health, maker, goodness, truth, and dwelling place.[17] In metaphorical speech, David affirms God's role as creator and sovereign, savior and redeemer. He acknowledges his divine aseity, perfection, and covenant-keeping loyalty. He stands in awe of his

---

17 Psalms 3:3, 5:2, 7:17, 10:14, 16:5, 18:1-2, 18:13, 19:14, 23:1, 24:7-10, 27:1, 31:5, 43:4, 42:11, 46:1, 50:1, 59:9, 59:10, 61:2, 61:3, 62:7, 71:3, 73:26, 75:7, 78:35, 78:41, 84:4, 89:17, 90:1, 95:6, 109:1, 110:5-7, 118:14, 121:5, 144:2. According to Brenda B. Colijn, "If we allow a new metaphor to become part of our conceptual system, it can create a new reality for us by shaping our perceptions and guiding our future actions." Colijn argues that scriptural metaphors enable us to re-envision God, ourselves, and the world around us. She gives four reasons: 1) figurative language is more arresting than literal language; 2) images make abstract ideas easier to understand by expressing them in concrete terms; 3) images have an important role in forming and sustaining identity; 4) images are powerful vehicles for carrying a vision. Building on Colijn's analysis, David's psalm project can be viewed as a warrior guide to identity formation. His project, latent with metaphor, calls the warrior to re-envision his God, himself, and the world around him. It provides metaphor that will create and sustain the vision of being both a man of God and a man of war. Brenda B. Colijn, Images of Salvation in the New Testament (Downers Grove: IVP Academic, 2010), 18-20.

matchless power and perfect knowledge, and rests in his steady mercy and certain justice. He sings over his glory and brilliance, finds comfort in his unchanging character and relishes in his kindness and provision. These metaphors paint a picture of a man who knew and loved God.

Considering the metaphors in the Psalms, it is worth noting that many contain warrior themes: Lord of Hosts (84:3-4), warrior (110:5-7), deliverer (144:2), strength (18:1-2), shelter (61:3), strong tower (61:3), mighty God (50:1), shield (3:3), defense (59:9), help in trouble (46:1), buckler (18:2), fortress (18:2).[18] David did not compartmentalize his faith. His experience as a warrior informed his faith, and his faith drove his vocation. This is evident in the way that his language from the combat zone found its way into the Psalms, and the warrior language of the Psalms found its way

18 "The images of God used throughout the Psalter have a distinct 'homeland security' ring to them." Bailey references the metaphors shield, high tower, fortress, high place, refuge, rock, stronghold, and horn of salvation and states, "these images are presented together and have a powerful cumulative effect." Bailey, The Good Shepherd, 35. Jerome Creach argues that the entire Psalter is shaped around the motif of God as refuge. Jerome F.D. Creach, Yahweh as Refuge and the Editing of the Hebrew Psalter (Sheffield: Sheffield Academic Press, 1996), 122-126.

onto the field of battle.

David was not just an ordinary warrior, he was also a theologian. As highlighted above, the contours of his theology are discernible in his stories and songs. Through the narratives and poetry one can discern a number of critical theological axioms; here are four that are important in the warfighting vocation. First, he affirmed the transcendence and imminence of God; that is, he recognized the otherness of God while relishing in his nearness.[19] He knew the lofty status of God and the lowly posture he willingly took. He comfortably held these two theological truths in proper tension. For the warrior, proper fear of the high God along with confidence in His lowly solidarity are both combat critical perspectives.[20]

---

19 David speaks often of God's holiness, lofty dwelling, and utter uniqueness: Psalm 18:16, 20:6, 24:3, 29:2, 43:3, 47:8, 68:5, 92:8, 97:9, 104:13, 113:4. While affirming this high view of God, David also speaks of God's lowliness, stooping posture, and nearness: Psalm 34:18, 65:4, 69:18, 73:28, 75:1, 119:151, 138:6, 145:18, 148:14.

20 This theological dynamic gives the warrior a dual perspective on God in the midst of combat. God is high above. He is the holy judge to whom warfighters are accountable. He is to be feared, revered, and obeyed. At the very same time, God is profoundly humble as he comes low to meet us in the trenches. He is in the war zone; he is a combat medic with blood-stained hands, the battle-buddy that is not going

Second, David recognized the creator-creature distinction as he affirmed God's enthroned status and limitless power, his creative and sustaining presence behind all things juxtaposed with the dependence, trust, worship, and obedience fundamental to the creature.[21] From David's view, freedom and joy are found when life is lived within this framework. For the warrior, the creator-creature nexus is fundamental to the vocation. Accountability, dependence, humility, embracing mortality, affirming the image of God, assurance in death, confidence in the proper use of force all flow from this critical framework.[22]

---

anywhere. He is in the fray with the warrior, unimpeded by the mess, pain, and hell of warfare. Divine standards and divine solidarity flow from this framework.

21 David often speaks of God, the creator and sustainer of all life: Psalm 90:2, 95:5-6, 100:3, 102:18, 104:30, 148:15, 149:2. At the same time, he focuses on man as a dependent creature resting on God for existence: Psalm 8:4, 100:3, 104:30, 119:73, 139:13.

22 The creator-creature distinction is fundamental to right relationship with God. Notably, it is this distinction that was rejected in the fall (Gen 3:1-7, Rom 1:18-25). Right relating to God means affirming his rightful place while staying in ours. This posture provides accountability, proper dependence on God and rightful humility. It provokes gratitude for God's provision and protection. In Luther's discussion on the Apostle's Creed, he discusses the critical importance of affirming God's creator status and our creaturely position. Reflecting

# Third, David held the justice and love of God in

on the statement, "I believe in God the Father Almighty, maker of heaven and earth," Luther states, "I believe that God has created me together with all that exists. God has given me and still preserves my body and soul: eyes, ears, and all limbs and senses; reason and all mental faculties. In addition, God daily and abundantly provides shoes and clothing, food and drink, house and farm, spouse and children, fields, livestock, and all property—along with all the necessities and nourishment for this body and life. God protects me against all danger and shields and preserves me from all evil. And all this is done out of pure, fatherly, and divine goodness and mercy, without any merit or worthiness of mine at all! For all of this I owe it to God to thank and praise, serve and obey him. This is most certainly true." Martin Luther, Luther's Little Instruction Book: The Small Catechism of Martin Luther (Boulder: Project Gutenberg, 1994). This perspective also speaks to the gravity of combat for it is God alone who is the giver and taker of life. Brandishing the God-given sword entails standing in God's stead and fulfilling his purposes (Rom 13:1-7). Recognizing God as creator and sustainer of life pushes the warfighter to face his mortality, to be prepared for death. Right relationship with one's Maker is the only thing that can produce confidence in the face of one's final breath. Affirming one's own creature status along with everyone else involved in war is essential for warrior health. The image of God in man is a critical theological truth for warfighters. When affirmed, it upholds the dignity, value, and honor due to one's battle buddy, one's enemy, and even one's self. This conviction must set parameters for how combatants handle themselves in theater. Contrary to what some think, the affirmation of the image of God in human beings does not exclude the necessity of taking life. From a scriptural perspective, this high view of human beings actually grounds the act of taking life when justice dictates (Gen 9:5-6).

proper tension.[23] He refused to dichotomize these divine attributes but rather affirmed instead their intimate relationship. He spoke of a fierce, unreserved love of God for His people, for the oppressed, and for the nations. Then, in the same breath, he could speak of an unwavering posture of justice toward sin, wrongdoing, and rebellion. This tension is essential for warfighter theology. It equips a warrior to think deeply about two seemingly contrary principles at work in his vocation. Exploring this tension helps him navigate the morally treacherous terrain of loving one's neighbor, loving one's enemy, and the vocational necessity of taking life.[24]

---

23 Love was a major theme in David's songs, mentioned at least 164 times: Psalms 5:7, 6:4, 13:5, 21:7, 26:3, 31:7, 36:5. Justice was equally important: Psalms 9:7, 10:18, 33:5, 37:6, 28, 82:3, 97:2, 101:1. In the character of God, love and justice meet together and dwell intimately side by side (Ex 34:6-7; Ps 85:10). D.A. Carson does an excellent job showing how the love and justice of God coinhere. D.A. Carson, The Difficult Doctrine of the Love of God (Wheaton, IL: Crossway Books, 2000), 65-84.

24 The warrior is called like any other follower of Christ to love God, love neighbor, and love one's enemy. He is also called to love justice, leave justice in the hands of God, and entrust justice to the governing authorities appointed by God. His unique vocational setting, however, places him in the realm of those appointed to execute justice. A thoroughgoing understanding of public and private requirements

Fourth, David embodied and taught the rhythm of obedience and repentance.[25] A listening ear and obedient heart were the pursuit of David, demonstrated by his commitment to honoring God and doing his will. Yet at his best, he knew broken obedience was all he had to offer. As ferociously as David pursued obedience, he chased repentance. In his brokenness and failure, David owned his sin and sought the mercy of God.[26] This

---

of executing justice, a grasp of eternal and temporal justice, and comprehending how justice and love are truly enmeshed are essential for warfighter health.

25 David sought a life of obedience before God: Psalm 18:21, 38:20, 40:6-8, 119:1-176. David also owned his brokenness and lived a life of repentance before God: 2 Samuel 12:1-14; Psalm 25:18, 32:1-7, 51:1-17.

26 "The David of the census story is a person of confession and supplication par excellence, a human sinner who repents, and seeks forgiveness." Ralph W. Klein, "David: Sinner and Saint in Samuel and Chronicles," Currents in Theology and Mission 26, no. 2 (1999): 104, 116. "It is not that David is sinless that makes him a model, but rather that this great sinner, who trusted in the exceedingly great mercies of God, confessed his sins and followed through on divinely prescribed obligations of repentance." Daniel Gard provides four observations about David's life of repentance: "1) the grace of God that extended to the sinner David is precisely that known from the continuing theological narrative of the canon: the objective justification of the world; 2) repentance requires the acknowledgement of personal responsibility; 3) the call to repentance, while a gracious call to all people, is especially a call to those who have been placed in positions

rhythm is important for warrior health. Obedience to God's commands is crucial on every level for those in the profession of arms. At the same time, failure is inevitable. In a combat setting, however, the stakes of moral failure are tremendous. Repentance is a balm for those dealing in life and death situations, facing moral injury, carrying guilt, harboring shame, and wrestling with unforgiveness.[27]

---

of leadership among the people of God; 4) whenever sin is forgiven by God, it is truly forgiven." Daniel L. Gard, "The Chronicler's David: Saint and Sinner," Concordia Theological Quarterly 70 (2006): 251-252. Larson and Zust argue that confession and repentance are essential mechanisms in moving morally injured warriors toward health, freedom, and hope. Duane Larson and Jeff Zust, Care for the Sorrowing Soul: Healing Moral Injuries from Military Service and Implications for the Rest of Us (Eugene: Cascade Books, 2017), 195-202. See also, Gary Knoppers, "Images of David in Early Judaism: David as Repentant Sinner in Chronicles" Biblica. 76, no. 4 (1995): 469.

27 For Christian combatants, the warrior code is already written. Adherence to the commands, principles, and wisdom of God forms their ethical posture. Understanding God's Word is essential for the warrior ethos. Recognition of human frailty, sinfulness, and inevitable failure is a necessity for solid warfighter theology. The gift and mechanism of repentance must be understood and utilized for warrior wellness. There are interior wounds that will not be handled apart from repentance, God's skillful soul-care, and his provision of forgiveness. David is an excellent model of fierce repentance. Notably, the most prominent story of his repentance was in a warfighting context (2 Sam 11-12; Ps 51). This

Healthy warriors are theologians: they are training their minds and hearts toward a vision of God that will ground, balance, and sustain them in their vocation. They do the hard work of holding converse theological truths together that breathe life into their unique settings. They intentionally infuse their theology with combat experience and allow their theology to drive their warfighting. Like David's, their relationship with God is their lifeline.

will be covered further in the section on the "Godly Warfighter's Sin, Shame and Guilt."

# 3

# The Warrior's Understanding of War

In the narratives of David, readers see extensive combat experience, and are able to discern how he engages his God in the midst of it. But does Scripture speak to David's view of war? What does he think about combat? How does he process it? How does it intersect with his faith? David does not provide an account of his thinking on the issue, but the reader can piece together fragments of his thinking through his written material.

For David, everything about warfighting was spiritual. In his context, some of the wars he fought were sanctioned by God (2 Sam 5:19). Yet, many wars were not explicitly sanctioned (2 Sam 10:4-14). In both scenarios, David operated the same way. He sought

God before going to battle (1 Sam 23:1-5), depended on God in the midst of battle (1 Sam 17:44-49), and gave God the credit at the end of battle (2 Sam 5:20). David recognized that his combat training, ability, and effectiveness did not originate from him. For David, God is the trainer of hands and fingers for battle (Ps 144:1; 2 Sam 22:35). It is God who enables speed, agility, and courage to attack in combat (Ps 18:29; 2 Sam 22:30, 34). He fought with the knowledge that his God was a warrior, the Lord of Armies who battled for him (Ps 24:8-10). He knew victory did not come from numbers, technology, or expertise but from the hand of God (1 Sam 17:46-47; Ps 20:7, 33:16-17).[28]

As a student of the biblical law, David was well

---

28 "In, with, and through the narrative of 1 Samuel 17, a theological thrust is conveyed, that the outcome of all battles depends upon God, no matter what the stature, resources, or experience possessed by the warring entities." Abraham Kuruvilla, "David v. Goliath (1 Samuel 17): What is the Author Doing with what He is Saying?" Journal of the Evangelical Theological Society 58, no. 3 (2015): 506. Robert Chisholm states, "The warriors Jonathan and David recognize that Yahweh alone determines the outcome of the battle. Soldiers and weapons have no impact on the outcome when Yahweh is involved (1 Sam 14:6; 17:47)." Robert B. Chisholm Jr., "Yahweh's Self Revelation in Deed and Word: A Biblical Theology of 1-2 Samuel," Southwestern Journal of Theology 55, no. 2 (2013): 225.

versed in the war guidance of Deuteronomy 20 along with the pre- and post-war rituals woven through the Old Testament.[29] These spiritual practices would likely have been implemented in his approach to warfare. Further, God's commands given in the Mosaic Law provided accountability and parameters within which combatants must operate for the sake of their brothers in arms, their families, their enemies, and themselves.[30]

29 Wood argues that Deuteronomy 20 prefigures the contours of just war thinking. Such principles informed David's warfighting. John Wood, Perspectives on War in the Bible (Macon, GA: Mercer University Press, 1998), 147-151.

30 As mentioned above, the Scripture provides the foundation for the Christian's warrior code. Susan French rightly argues that the warrior code protects the humanity of warfighters and all those connected to them, even their enemies. "The code of the warrior not only defines how warriors should interact with their own warrior comrades, but also how they should treat other members of their society, their enemies, and the people they conquer. The code restrains the warrior. It sets boundaries on acceptable behavior. It distinguishes honorable acts from shameful acts…warriors need the restraint of a warrior's code to keep them from losing their humanity and their ability to enjoy a life worth living outside the realm of combat." Susan E. French, "The Code of the Warrior: Ideals of Warrior Cultures Throughout History," The Journal of Character & Leadership Integration (2017): 65, 67. In another work, French explores key warrior cultures through history and how they imbued their warfighters with combat values. In every culture and period of history, a warrior code has been essential for safeguarding men and women in arms along with their communities. Susan E. French, The Code of

War drove David to God; it placed him in a position of desperation and dependence. It regularly placed him on his knees for wisdom, help, and strength. It sharpened his theological grasp of God, himself, and the world around him. It pushed him to lean on the community of faith for support and stability. It forced him to get comfortable with mortality and to live with death at his back. For David, war was a catalyst to move the warrior toward his Creator.

David's spiritual framework for war did not exempt him from its horrors. David was haunted by his experiences, and, as a man of blood, he knew well the inevitable trauma that chases the warrior. His enemies were never far from his mind. When pouring out his heart to God, the Psalms reveal expressions of despair, sorrow, guilt, shame, fear, anxiety, and grief. As a leader, his combat losses weighed heavily on his soul.

His war experiences hit close to home on numerous occasions. He knew what it was like to have his home destroyed in the midst of war (1 Sam 30:1-3), to lose family members to violent conflict (2 Sam 18:15, 33),

the Warrior: Exploring Warrior Values Past and Present (New York: Rowman & Littlefield Publishers, 2003).

to have his family torn apart because of war (2 Sam 15:13-37; 1 Sam 30:1-3), and to experience the impact of war on being a husband and father (2 Sam 11-15). While never physically wounded in battle, David did not walk away unscathed. He bore the moral wounds of combat until the day of his death.[31]

---

31 Chris Adsit frames David as a PTSD sufferer based on the lament psalms. He argues that David is the template for healing the wounds of combat trauma. Utilizing the psalms as a paradigm, he suggests a number of select prayers, promises, and praises for the wounded warrior on the journey toward wellness. Though Adsit's position reaches beyond the biblical data, his observation of the combat impact on David's life is sound. Chris Adsit, The Combat Trauma Healing Manual: Christ-centered Solutions for Combat Trauma (Newport News: Military Ministry Press, 2007), 165-170. Grimell's intriguing work forms a dialogue between combat trauma research and biblical studies. She states, "insights can be gained into how different biblical characters handled their darker war selves and deplored actions, their potential moral and/or spiritual injuries in relation to God and others, their commitment to military purpose, loyalty to unit and battle buddies, and their difficulties in readjustment after combat." She suggests that David was an "extremely resilient veteran" and yet there were a number of combat experiences and decisions that illustrated "potential moral injury events." Grimell, "Contemporary Insights from Biblical Combat Veterans," 242, 244-245. Tick states, "David has been called a 'PTSD sufferer' but also, in contrast to Saul, a 'PTSD victor.' His life was replete with personal, familial and historical traumas. He was involved in betrayals, murders, infidelity, incest and conflicts with his children unto making war son upon father. His Psalms reveal a man, warrior and king in confusion, despair, loneliness and spiritual collapse. They also reveal a person of deep faith who sometimes felt Divine presence and favor, in

David's perspective on war combines realism with faith. He did not downplay the dread of war or minimize its fallout. He was honest about combat's impact on his soul, his family, and his colleagues. At the same time, he infused his view of war with faith and spirituality. His training, pre-war rituals, experience in combat, and post-war practices were all executed before the face of God. This interface of realism and faith produced a rugged, resilient warrior.[32]

---

distress sought its renewal, and through life gave it praise. David's invisible wound sang through his flood of anguished poetry and sounded a relentless appeal for Divine help." Edward Tick, Warrior's Return: Restoring the Soul after War (Boulder: Sounds True, 2014), 111-115.

32 David Bosworth argues that the narratives of 1-2 Samuel characterize David as a resilient individual. Defining resilience as an individual's "capacity to continue with their lives more or less as normal in spite of trauma, loss, or other adversity that might be expected to result in significant dysfunction." Focusing on the death of Bathsheba's firstborn, Bosworth concludes, "the resilient faith that David displays in this incident is consistent with the depiction of his character elsewhere. David frequently demonstrates his resilient faith in God in times of adversity. He invokes pious motives for preferring to endure adversity rather than kill Saul (1 Sam 24:7; 26:9-11) or Shimei (2 Sam 16:12)." David A. Bosworth, "Faith and Resilience: King David's Reaction to the Death of Bathsheba's Firstborn," The Catholic Biblical Quarterly 73 (2011): 692, 706.

# 4

# The Warrior's Attitude
# toward the Enemy

One of David's most significant contributions to warfighter theology is his complex understanding and relationship to his enemies, an issue that is ever relevant to warriors of all eras. Enemies are a pervasive theme throughout 1-2 Samuel, at times, they seem omnipresent as they dominate the landscape of David's story.[33]

The Psalms speak regularly to this theme as well,

---

33 1 Sam 17:40-54; 18:6-13, 28-29; 19:2, 9-17; 20:30-34; 21:10; 22:16-22; 23:1-29; 24:1-22; 25:20-21; 26:1-25; 27:8-12; 28:1-2; 29:4; 30:1-30; 2 Sam 1:11-12; 2:12-32; 3:1; 5:17-25; 7:9; 8:1-14; 10:1-19; 11:1, 14-17; 12:26-31; 15:13-18; 16:7-9, 21-23; 17:1-29; 18:1-18; 19:18-23; 20:4-22; 21:1-5, 15-22; 22:4, 18-19, 38-43; 23:8-23; 1 Kgs 2:5-9.

104 of 150 Psalms reference enemies.[34] This is a staggering and often overlooked data point from the book of Psalms. That 70 percent of Israel's prayer book is concerned with enemies must change the way the book is read. The abundance of material on David's engagement with his enemies is a rich resource for training the conscience and character of today's warrior.

David's posture toward his enemies is far from one-dimensional; rather, his approach is layered and multi-faceted. He models the complexity a godly warrior must embrace to navigate the enemy dynamic. David's disposition toward his enemies has four anchor points: affirm dignity, execute justice, leave vengeance to God, and show mercy and forgiveness. This disposition is captured in the graphic below.

---

34 "The Psalms bristle with talk about enemies." Marti J. Steussy, "The Enemy in the Psalms," Word & World 28, no. 1 (2008): 5. Martin Slabbert states, "Any person who would like to come to a better understanding of the Psalms, needs to take the relationship between the pious and the enemy into account." Martin J. Slabbert, "Coping in a harsh reality: The concept of the 'enemy' in the composition of Psalms 9 and 10," HTS Theological Studies 71, no. 3 (2015): 1. Erhard Gerstenberger states, "The Psalter, it is true, does speak a great deal about enemies and evildoers." Erhard S. Gerstenberger, "Enemies and Evildoers in the Psalms: A Challenge to Christian Preaching," Horizons in Biblical Theology 4, no. 5 (1983): 61.

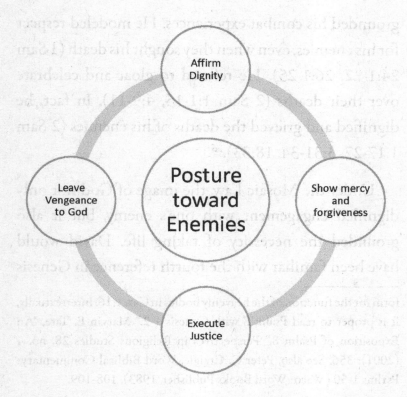

The first anchor is David's affirmation of the inherent dignity of his enemies. David's understanding of creation informed his view on human-beings, both friend and foe. The image of God undergirded David's anthropology (Ps 8:5-8).[35] This theological affirmation

35 "This dominion-having of humanity is different from that in Genesis 1, but it is close enough to attract the attention of almost all interpreters. There is no 'image of God' for humanity in Psalm 8, but the near-divine status, followed by the declaration of divinely given rulership, is taken to be equivalent. The verb for rule, is used in a noun

grounded his combat experiences. He modeled respect for his enemies, even when they sought his death (1 Sam 24:1-22, 26:1-25). He refused to gloat and celebrate over their deaths (2 Sam 1:1-15, 4:9-11). In fact, he dignified and grieved the deaths of his enemies (2 Sam 1:17-27, 3:31-34, 18:33).[36]

Under the Mosaic Law, the image of God not only dignified engagement with one's enemy, but it also grounded the necessity of taking life. David would have been familiar with the fourth reference in Genesis

form for the function of the heavenly bodies in Gen 1:16. Intertextually, it is proper to read Psalm 8 with Genesis 1-2." Marvin E. Tate, "An Exposition of Psalm 8," Perspectives in Religious Studies 28, no. 4 (2001): 356. See also, Peter C. Craigie, Word Biblical Commentary: Psalms 1-50 (Waco: Word Books Publisher, 1983), 108-109.

36 The narratives of David make clear that David did not always live up to this facet of the biblical warrior code. His callous murder of one of his best soldiers is case in point. He failed to affirm the imago dei in this warrior. Instead, he takes the life of a friend, not foe, and expresses no grief over his death (2 Sam 11:25). David's engagement with Nabal demonstrates his dark-side. The narrative models the potential of vengeance overriding the dignity-affirming response to one's enemy (1 Sam 25:1-39). The stories of David beg other important questions in this vein: Was dismembering the bodies of enemies something prescribed by God or a moral infringement by David (1 Sam 17:51)? David's seething resentment and vengeance toward his enemies is revealed on his death-bed: his final wish includes the death of two individuals. How does this square with this perspective (1 Kgs 2:5-9)?

to the image of God: "Whoever sheds the blood of man, by man shall his blood be shed, for God made man in His own image (Gen 9:6)." The image of God asserts the utter dignity of mankind, which includes accountability.[37] Justice affirms value, it speaks to moral agency, and it refuses to treat human beings as anything other than image-bearers.[38]

---

37 "Gen 9:6 empowers humanity to return blood for blood and justifies retributive violence by appealing to humanity's creation in the image of God. Humans, in other words, violently punish bloodshed because we are made in God's image, and by doing so we imitate God's actions in the flood." Stephen M. Wilson, "Blood Vengeance and the Imago Dei in the Flood Narrative (Genesis 9:6)," Interpretation: A Journal of Bible and Theology 71, no. 3 (2017): 265. According to Daniel Weiss, the rabbinic interpretation of Genesis 9:6 follows this line of thought, "the classical rabbinic understanding of the image of God as the living and embodied human individual represents a profound challenge to modern assumptions about bloodshed and violence on both the individual and collective levels." Daniel H. Weiss, "Direct divine sanction, the prohibition of bloodshed, and the individual as image of God in classical rabbinical literature," Journal of the Society of Christian Ethics 32, no. 2 (2012): 33.

38 Wilson argues that the flood narrative has a new creation motif. With the reset of creation comes the call to be "fruitful and multiply" (Gen 9:1, 7). Notably, the imperatives to "rule and subdue the earth" (Gen 1:28) found in the original creation story are absent. Wilson argues that ensuring justice is the new "rule and subdue." He states, "Their conspicuous absence here strongly suggests that the action incumbent on humanity as God's vice-regent outlined at the end of the flood narrative—namely, to avenge innocent shed blood—replaces the

The image of God has two implications for enemy engagement. Both are essential for the well-being of the warfighter. Warriors need safeguards against the soul-wounding tendency of dehumanization.[39] This doctrine

depiction of the imago Dei from the creation story in light of the divine reassessment of creation after the flood." Wilson, "Blood Vengeance and the Imago Dei," 272.

39 "It's so much easier to kill someone if they look distinctly different from you. If your propaganda machine can convince your soldiers that their opponents are not really humans but are 'inferior forms of life,' then their natural resistance to killing their own species will be reduced." David Grossman, On Killing: The Psychological Costs of Learning to Kill in War and Society (New York: Back Bay Books, 2009), 35. Emile Bruneau asserts the principle that "wars begin in the minds of men." In order to subdue the "strong moral prohibitions and psychological restraints against harming others," nations have leveraged the dehumanization of other groups. Taking the holocaust as test-case, the article asserts, "Many psychologists suggested that the horror committed by the Nazis against Jews, the Roma and others was enabled by the perception of these groups as 'sub-human', which led to 'moral disengagement' from their suffering." Emile Bruneau and Nour Kteily, "The enemy as animal: Symmetric dehumanization during asymmetric warfare," Plos One, 12, no. 7 (2017): 1. According to Susan French, "Propaganda that tries to deny the humanity of enemies and associate them with subhuman animals is a common and effective tool for increasing aggression and breaking down the resistance to killing. This dehumanization can be achieved through the use of animal imagery and abusive language." She asserts further, "The act of dehumanizing, both in the context of war and psychological experiments, is strongly associated with psychological trauma." Susan E. French, "Dehumanizing the Enemy: The Intersection of

provides this protection in two ways. First, it equips the uniform-wearer to affirm an enemy's inherent value in life and death: to see him as someone's son, husband, father and friend. In turn, it enables the warfighter to resist degrading his enemy's humanity in thought, speech, or action.[40] Second, it readies a warrior to

Neuroethics and Military Ethics" in Responsibilities to Protect: Perspectives in Theory and Practice, ed. David Whetham and Bradley J. Strawser (Boston: Brill Nijhoff, 2015), 176-177. Robert Stroud asserts, "You see, the horrible irony is that in dehumanizing the enemy, we also dehumanize ourselves…demonizing our enemies is not only an offense against truth; it is destructive to our national and personal soul." Robert C. Stroud, "Demonizing Our Enemies & Dehumanizing Ourselves," Curtana Sword of Mercy 54 (2009): 54-57.

40 "There is an intimate connection between the psychological health of the veteran and the respect he feels for those he fought… restoring honor to the enemy is an essential step in recovery from combat PTSD." Further, French argues that "by setting standards of behavior for themselves, accepting certain restraints, and even 'honoring their enemies,' warriors can create a lifeline that will allow them to pull themselves out of the hell of war and reintegrate themselves into their society, should they survive to see peace restored." This principle also applies to warriors "who fight from a distance— who drop bombs or shoot missiles from planes or ships or submarines"; they are also in danger of "losing their humanity." For these warriors, "what threatens them is the very ease by which they can take lives. As technology separates individuals from the results of their actions, it cheats them of the chance to absorb and reckon with the enormity of what they have done." French, "The Code of the Warrior," 68. Kevin Sites illustrates through the stories of combatants that men do not

hold image-bearers accountable for their actions. It ensures the vocational combatant that within certain boundaries taking life does not diminish human dignity but upholds it.[41]

This dual-pronged paradigm informs every other area of thinking about enemies in the material regarding

come back whole who have not come to terms with their enemies. He shows that for many, the path to healing is directly linked to facing how they have viewed and what they have done to their enemies. Kevin Sites, The Things They Cannot Say (New York: Harper Perennial, 2013), 165-182. For Luther, the doctrine of vocation and the dignity of warfighting also provides a safeguard against dehumanizing one's enemy. "While some believe that dehumanizing one's enemy is the only way in which one can 'mentally' prepare soldiers for the serious and psychologically traumatic act of killing a fellow human being, Luther need not take this route due to his understanding of being a soldier as a godly vocation in and through which God himself is at work. The soldier as the government's and, therefore, God's agent is elevated to high honors in this way; consequently, his enemy need not be degraded to a subhuman level." Martin Luther, Christians Can Be Soldiers (Minneapolis: Lutheran Press, 2010), 106.

41 "Such tremendous strife, common throughout the entire world, which no one can endure, must be counteracted by the little strife called war or the sword. This is why God honors the sword so highly that he calls it his own order. God does not want us to say or think that humans invented or established it. Because of this, the hand that uses this sword and kills is no longer man's hand, but God's hand. In such a case, it is not man, but God, who hangs, tortures, beheads, slays, and wars. All these are his works and judgments." Luther, "Christians Can Be Soldiers," 17.

David. It rests in the background in the following discussions on executing justice, leaving vengeance to God, and forgiving one's enemies. In contemporary practice, a warrior would do well to allow this framework to drive one's philosophy and praxis of enemy engagement.

The execution of justice is the second anchor point informing David's approach to his enemies. As discussed above, this principle builds on the inherent dignity and accountability of image-bearing enemies. As a leader and warrior, David saw protection for his people as paramount. He ruled a nation that was surrounded on all sides by enemies. Safety required combat.

In the stories of David, there is a moral boundary between protective/responsive combat and unwarranted/vengeful violence.[42] David had no qualms about engaging in combat when his people were in danger (1 Sam 30:1-17). However, engagement in battle for unjust reasons resulted in guilt, judgment,

---

42 The biblical data is admittedly more complex. The presence of divinely commanded war is another category in these narratives. Amidst the narrative layers, the reader must discern contemporary discontinuity and continuity. In David's journey, there are a number of battles that are not divinely sanctioned, at least explicitly. In this sphere of war, godly principles and wisdom informed David's approach. In particular, it appears that David was well aware of what constituted a just and unjust response to conflict

and a damaged conscience (1 Sam 25:1-39).[43]

The third anchor point for David's posture toward his enemies is leaving vengeance to God. There are

---

43 The Nabal/Abigail narrative is rich with warfighter theology (1 Sam 25:1-39). David is tempted to engage Nabal's folly with vengeance and bloodshed. On the verge of wiping out an entire tribe, Abigail shrewdly restrains David. Her persuasive speech includes warnings of God's judgment, self-injury and heavy guilt for wrongful vengeance. Abigail's language includes "bloodguilt" (25:26), "saving with your own hand" (25:26, 31) and being spared from "grief or pangs of conscience for having shed blood without cause" (25:31). David follows Abigail's counsel and praises her for restraining him from "bloodguilt" (25:33) and working salvation with his "own hand" (25:33). Ralph Klein notes that the Nabal/Abigail narrative falls between two episodes where David spares the life of Saul (1 Sam 24, 26). The narrator is providing a stark contrast of David's behavior in those stories and his desire for vengeance in this narrative. Klein links the language of salvation by one's "own hand" to a flawed combat endeavor in Deuteronomy 20:4 (cf. Josh 7:2). Ralph W. Klein, Word Biblical Commentary: 1 Samuel, (Waco: Word Books Publisher, 1983), 250. According to Walter Brueggemann, the narrative demonstrates David's "dangerous potential and 'near surface' destructiveness." Bruggemann rightly asserts, "Had it not been for Abigail, David would have done in both Nabal and himself." Walter Brueggemann, Interpretation, A Biblical Commentary for Teaching and Preaching: First and Second Samuel (Louisville: John Knox Press, 1990), 175, 180. Clearly, there are parameters within which a warfighter must operate to preserve his conscience before God. The language in the story points to the destructive force of wrongful violence on one's relationship with God, one's neighbor, and one's self. If there were ever a biblical prelude to the contemporary moral injury discussion this would be it.

numerous examples of David's refusal to take matters into his own hands when encountering his enemies (1 Sam 24:1-22, 26:1-25; 2 Sam 16:5-13). "May the Lord avenge the wrongs you have done to me, but my hand will not touch you" captures the sentiment of David in these scenarios (1 Sam 24:12, 25:39, 26:10).

The Psalms embody this dynamic in David's life. As mentioned earlier, the language about enemies is pervasive in the Psalms. David did not leave his combat experiences, fear for his life, and desire for victory over his enemies out of worship. Instead, the reader finds vengeance psalms dominating his communication with God. Such prominence has merited the distinct category of the imprecatory psalm.

David does not restrain his emotions or harsh intentions toward his enemies. Instead, he gives full vent to them before the face of God. In a bold act of faith, David abdicates his own vengeance while entrusting himself to the just action of the Almighty.[44] For David,

---

44 "David did not react in private revenge, as might be expected in such a circumstance. Instead, he released the retaliatory demands of justice to the One in whose jurisdiction it rightfully lies." Day argues that "at times it is legitimate for God's people to utter prayers of imprecation or pleas for divine vengeance—like those in the Psalms… these prayers are a divinely appointed source of power for believers in their powerlessness. In the face of sustained injustice, hardened enmity, and gross oppression, they are the Christians' hope that divine

the warrior must live naked before God. Soul wellness
for the warfighter requires moral rigor within a covenant

---

justice will indeed be realized—not only in the eschaton (2 Thess. 1:6-
10)." John N. Day, "The Imprecatory Psalms and Christian Ethics,"
Bibliotheca Sacra 159 (2002): 175, 185-186. According to Dominic
Hankle, "When one submits to God by praying a curse he or she is
no longer free to take revenge, because vengeance is transferred
from the heart of the speaker to God, who plays an interested
role in the believer's life. Although at first this sounds as if one is
advocating that God will be a destroying force to call upon, in reality
it leaves responsibility in God's hands to make right what appears so
wrong." Dominic D. Hankle, "The Therapeutic Implications of the
Imprecatory Psalms in the Christian Counseling Setting," Journal
of Psychology and Theology 38, no. 4 (2010): 278. Anderson states,
"The plea for God to take vengeance on evildoers is not merely a call
for personal and perhaps therefore petty revenge. It is rather a prayer
that God underscore a principle fundamental to all human society:
that good behavior will be rewarded and evil behavior punished. The
imprecatory language of the Psalmist is so impassioned because the
very concept of justice itself is at stake." Further, Anderson follows
Gregory of Nyssa's thought as he argues that the "imprecatory psalms
give witness to that deep abyss of personal hatred that David, through
divine grace, was able to overcome." Anderson, "King David and the
Psalms of Imprecation," 270, 272. Gerstenberger emphasizes the need
for utilizing imprecatory psalms in a corporate setting as a source of
accountability and communal healing. "Enemies are now being treated
not simply eye to eye in a deadly group-conflict, but in the presence of a
supreme judge." Gerstenberger, "Enemies and Evildoers in the Psalms,"
77. See also, Martin J. Ward, "Psalm 109: David's Poem of Vengeance,"
Andrews University Seminary Studies 28, no. 2 (1980): 166-167.

# relationship with God.[45]

45 Brueggemann uses the language of "covenant partnership" to describe the divine-human relationship. Covenant with God is an invitation to rugged authenticity and fierce transparency about all of life. He argues that imprecatory psalms are "unguarded language that in most religious discourse is censored…this is the voice of resentment and vengeance that will not be satisfied until God works retaliation on those who have done wrong…in these psalms of disorientation one speaks unguardedly about how it in fact is. The stunning fact is that Israel does not purge this unguardedness but regards it as genuinely faithful communication." Walter Brueggemann, The Message of the Psalms: A Theological Commentary (Minneapolis: Augsburg, 1985), 55. According to Steussy, "The psalms suggest that we should come honestly before God with how we do feel rather than wearing a brave mask of how we ought to feel…another reason for opening ourselves to our negative feelings is that this is usually the most effective way to get past them." Steussy, "The Enemy in the Psalms," 8. Hankle asserts, "Studies indicate that intentionally holding back emotions can cause harm to those who experience traumatic events…intentional withholding of emotional responses as a means to cope with combat trauma is uniquely associated with symptoms of post-traumatic stress disorder." Imprecatory psalms give combat veterans a mechanism for processing their experiences, suffering, and rage. "This form of prayer affirms that God hears the cry of those he loves and wants them to express in their terms the pain and suffering they feel. Yet, God is the one who administers justice so the client must develop a trusting relationship with God allowing him to take ownership of the situation. This ownership does not mean the resolution of the situation will be what one expects, but rather what God will do given his infinite knowledge of the complexity of the situation." Hankle, "The Therapeutic Implications of the Imprecatory Psalms," 277, 279. Wayne Ballard argues that the psalms of lament and imprecation are essential

The fourth and final anchor point for David's engagement with his enemies is mercy and forgiveness. While David called down God's vengeance on his enemies and executed justice with his own hands, he also extended love and forgiveness toward his enemies (1 Sam 24:1-22, 25:24-35, 26:1-25; 2 Sam 14:25-33, 19:18-23).[46] At times, former enemies became reconciled friends (2 Sam 3:6-21). David's love for his enemies was expressed in grief and honor at their deaths (2 Sam 1:17-27, 3:31-34, 18:33).

---

for those who desire peace and long to be peacemakers. He finds great utility in the full array of Psalms for contemporary challenges faced today. Wayne H. Ballard Jr., "Reading the Psalms in Light of 9-11: The Dialectic of War and Peace as Leitmotif in the Psalms of Ascents," Perspectives in Religious Studies 31, no. 4 (2004): 442-450. David Barshinger explores Jonathan Edward's view of the topic, "Edwards's interpretation suggests that Christians can read, pray, and sing these texts within the wider spectrum of God's work in the world." David P. Barshinger, "Spite or Spirit? Jonathan Edwards on the Imprecatory Language of the Psalms," Westminster Theological Journal 77 (2015): 69.

46 Speaking to the narrative of David's grief over Absalom, Eugene Merrill states, "Joab, completely disgusted by this show of emotion, reproached David, reminding him that time after time he had mourned for his enemies when he should have rejoiced at their defeat and death. First it was Saul, then Abner, then Ishbosheth, and now his own iniquitous son. If David possessed one overriding fault, in Joab's sight that fault was an irresponsible love for all men including his enemies (II Sam. 19:6)." Eugene H. Merrill, An Historical Survey of the Old Testament (Ada: Baker Academic, 1992), 222.

How loving one's enemy and waging war against him can coincide has been debated throughout church history.[47] In reality, conceptualizing such a coexistence is

47 Augustine argued that "the love of enemy command (as well as the commandment to not resist an evildoer) refers to an inner disposition, and not outward actions." Other theologians like Niebuhr argued that "fighting a war against our enemies is actually a way of loving them. While just war theory would support the idea that killing our enemy during a war may be a morally good thing, it seems disingenuous to maintain that it is still a method of loving them. Perhaps killing the person may prevent a greater evil that they might do, if they were allowed to go on living. Yet killing them is still tragic. Though it may be the lesser of two evils, it is still an evil. It is not one of many ways to love one's enemy, but rather the grieved admission that it is no longer possible to love that enemy right now." Johnston asserts that the "commandment to love our enemies should prevent us from committing two grave sins commonly associated with war. The first is the tendency to claim that God is on our side. The second is the tendency to dehumanize the enemy. In both of these sins, we deny our faith in a God whose love is so limitless that it extends even to our enemies." Laurie Johnston, "'Love Your Enemies' Even in the Age of Terrorism," Political Theology 6, no. 1 (2005): 93, 99. Mark Coppenger argues that loving one's enemy takes on a different form in war. He suggests that "one might enter into combat with a general sense that he is doing the enemy good by preventing him from accomplishing something awful... for love is not essentially a matter of feeling. It is instead a dogged commitment to what is best for the other, however, you may feel." Mark Coppenger, "The Golden Rule and War," Criswell Theological Review 4, no. 2 (1990): 306-307. Luther states, "What is war other than the punishing of injustice and evil? Why is war waged unless peace and obedience are desired? Even if killing and destroying

much cleaner than its actual expression.[48] Nonetheless, Scripture is quite comfortable with theological tension. The imperative to love one's enemy exists alongside the God-ordained work of bearing the sword. The call to love and protect one's neighbor is held together with the demand to turn the other cheek.[49] The peacemaking

do not seem like works of love, they are in reality nothing else." Luther, "Christians Can Be Soldiers," 14.

48 Alan Kirk argues that enemy love divorced from concrete social action dwindles into sentimentality. Enemy love is easy to talk about, much harder to put into solid action. Alan Kirk, "'Love your enemies' the Golden Rule, and ancient reciprocity (Luke 6:27-35)," Journal of Biblical Literature 122, no. 4 (2003): 686. French states, "Troops should not be asked to love their enemies while inflicting suffering and death upon them. This is the mindset of an abuser, not a mindset we wish to encourage in troops who will return to civilian life." French, "Dehumanizing the Enemy," 51.

49 "Forgiveness and vengeance exist side-by-side in the Bible, as they literally do in God's own self-revelation in Exod 34:7, where God identifies as one 'keeping steadfast love for the thousandth generation, forgiving iniquity and transgression and sin, yet by no means clearing the guilty, but visiting the iniquity of the parents upon the children and the children's children, to the third and the fourth generation.' This dichotomy likewise persists in the New Testament, where alongside the depiction of Jesus commanding love for enemies (Luke 6:27-29, 35) stands the image of the vengeful Christ riding a white horse and 'making war' against his foes (Rev 19:11- 21)." Wilson, "Blood Vengeance and the Imago Dei," 273. Serge Ruzer traces the call to love one's enemy back to Leviticus 19:8. He shows how the New Testament leverages this text on multiple occasions to inform enemy-love (Matt

mission of the church is affirmed along with the call to pursue justice. After all, discipleship is about following behind one who is both lion and lamb.

Vocational excellence and spiritual health in the profession of arms are contingent on the proper posture toward the enemy. Combat stress, moral injury, shame, guilt, remorse, grief, and the inverse of these are inextricably related to how warriors relate to their enemies.[50] David gives four anchor points that provide stability and safety for the vocational combatant. One-dimensional views of the enemy will not suffice; the warrior must have a layered view that includes the affirmation of dignity, the necessity of justice, the need to leave vengeance to God, and the call to mercy and forgiveness.

---

5:43-48; Lk 6:31-38; Rom 12:9-20). This dynamic demonstrates that this was not an alien concept to the old covenant believer. This is a tension that the people of God have grappled with for millennia. Serge Ruzer, "'Love Your Enemy' Precept in the Sermon on the Mount in the Context of Early Jewish Exegesis: A New Perspective," Revue Biblique 111, no. 2 (2004): 195, 208.

50 Jonathan Shay, Achilles in Vietnam: Combat Trauma and the Undoing of Character. (New York: Scribner, 1994), 103-119; Hankle, "The Therapeutic Implications of the Imprecatory Psalms," 275-279; French, "The Code of the Warrior," 66-70.

# 5

# The Warrior's Connection to Community

Healthy communities foster healthy warriors.[51] David knew this well. He was surrounded by a supportive community (1 Sam 18:16, 22:2). He loved gathering with his people for worship and ached for it when he was unable to do so (Pss 23:6, 26:8, 27:4, 69:9, 116:17-19, 122:1). He was part of a tight-knit band of brothers (2 Sam 23:8-39; 1 Sam 22:2),[52] had an inner

---

51 Susan French's research explores warrior cultures and how they shaped and cared for their fighters. She shows that healthy warriors come from healthy communities. Susan E. French, The Code of the Warrior: Exploring Warrior Values Past and Present (New York: Rowman & Littlefield Publishers, 2003), 10.

52 "We can therefore presume with considerable certainty, that a military elite of heroes was established while David was still the

circle of companions he could trust. (1 Sam 18:1-4, 19:1, 20:17, 23:16; 2 Sam 23:8-12),[53] and was surrounded by

captain of a band, and that this elite—the thirty warriors closest to the captain—had formed a kind of supreme command." Mazar further notes the diversity of the mighty men: "It becomes clear that thirteen out of the Thirty are from Bethlehem and its environs; five others are from various cities in the Judean mountains or from the families of Caleb in Southern Judaea; one is from Beth Ha'arabah in the Judean Desert near Jericho; and two are from the Northern Negeb (the tribe of Simon)…we should note that of these seven heroes one is an Ammonite; three, including the armor-bearer of Joab, are apparently of Hivvite origin; one is a Hittite; one a Hagarite (or a Gadhite); and one is of unknown origin. These seven were perhaps added on to the Thirty to serve as officers over foreign mercenary units in David's army. This occurred before the formation of the bodyguard (mishma'ath) comprised of the Kerethites and the Pelethites, a troop of Philistine origin commanded by Benaiah son of Jehoiada." This insight speaks to the bond that combat creates, a connection that cuts across race, culture, politics and economics. B. Mazar, "The Military Elite of King David," Vetus Testamentum 13, no. 3 (1963): 310, 318-319. See also, Moshe Garsiel, "David's Elite Warriors and their Exploits in the Books of Samuel and Chronicles," The Journal of Hebrew Scriptures 11 (2011): 2-28.

53 Patrcia Tull notes similarities between David and Jonathan's initial battle stories: "Each, armed with little more than valiance and faith, trounces stronger enemies, one need not wonder that he found in David a kindred spirit." Patricia K. Tull, "Jonathan's Gift of Friendship," Interpretation 58, no. 2 (2004): 134. According to Grimell, "David also cultivated deep friendships with battle buddies, for example Saul's son Jonathan; he and David developed a rare friendship and trust for each other." Grimell, "Contemporary Insights from Biblical Combat

a plethora of wise advisers (1 Chron 27:32-34; 1 Sam 25:23-31; 2 Sam 8:15-17, 12:1-13, 14:1-21).[54]

Israel was a warrior community, it knew the gravity of sending its men to fight (Deut 20:5-9) and the importance of bringing them home well (1 Sam 18:6-7; Num 31:19-20).[55] Collectively, the Israelite community absorbed the responsibility and consequences for its warfighters. Informed by the Mosaic rituals that prepared men for combat, empowered them in battle, and sought to return them whole, this community

---

Veterans," 246.

54 "The accounts in the books of Samuel and Kings suggest that the prophets Gad and Nathan brought divine messages or personal counsel to or for King David with some regularity and that their words were valued. Being concerned about the legitimacy and well-being of the king, Gad and Nathan are portrayed as counselor or crisis intervention specialists as well as transmitters of oracles." Dong-Young Yoon, "The Role of Prophets Gad and Nathan in the Davidic Court," Korean Journal of Christian Studies 109 (2018): 14. See also, Larry L. Lyke, King David with the Wise Woman of Tekoa: The Resonance of Tradition in Parabolic Narrative (Sheffield: Sheffield Academic, 1997), 186-193.

55 "Warfare was at the forefront of ancient Israel's consciousness and a brutal fact of life…the life of Israel is shaped amidst and punctuated by civil and international strive during the six centuries from the Exodus to the Exile." Wood, Perspectives on War in the Bible, 1.

knew how to take care of its own.[56]

Research bears out the critical importance of community at all levels for those in the profession of arms.[57] Strong relational connection is linked to trauma recovery.[58] Isolation, however, exacerbates the

---

56 1 Sam 7:9, 13:9-12, 21:5; 2 Sam 1:21, 11:11; Ex 15:1–18; Num 31:13-24, 48-54.

57 Jonathan Shay shows that connectedness at home, in one's unit and with one's larger community is essential for preventing and healing combat trauma. Home is the place where warriors know safety, acceptance, value, respect, familiarity, hope, and comfort. Warriors go to battle for home. In so doing, they often lose it as they are unraveled by trauma. Shay argues that preparation and restoration for warfighters is wrapped around this concept of home. Jonathan Shay, Odysseus in America: Combat Trauma and the Trials of Homecoming (New York: Scribner, 2002), 209-253. See also, Judith Herman, Trauma and Recovery: The aftermath of violence—from domestic abuse to political terror (New York: Basic Books, 1997), 61-73.

58 "The essential injuries in combat PTSD are moral and social, and so the central treatment must be moral and social. The best treatment restores control to the survivor and actively encourages communalization of the trauma." Tick, Warrior's Return, 119-139. "The proper relationship and implicit social contract between warriors and civilians are interchangeable concentric circles of protection and caring...this includes how any society uses its warriors, takes responsibility for their actions during and provides for their well-being afterward." Shay, Achilles in Vietnam, 187. Jim Rendon states, "Social support has been shown time and again to be a key factor in helping people recover from post-traumatic stress symptoms." Jim Rendon,

physical, mental, and spiritual complications of combat exposure.[59] David knew the protective and healing power of a worshipping community, a war-intelligent nation, close battle buddies, intimate friends, and wise counselors. His social support template for warfighter health is textbook, and it is an absolute must for military members today.

---

Upside: The New Science of Post-Traumatic Growth (New York: Touchstone, 2015), 84-102. See also, Larson and Zust, Care for the Sorrowing Soul, 202-208.

59 "A modern soldier returning from combat—or a survivor of Sarajevo—goes from the kind of close-knit group that humans evolved for, back into a society where most people work outside the home, children are educated by strangers, families are isolated from wider communities, and personal gain almost completely eclipses collective good. Even if he or she is part of a family, that is not the same as belonging to a group that shares resources and experiences almost everything collectively. Whatever the technological advances of modern society—and they're nearly miraculous—the individualized lifestyles that those technologies spawn seem to be deeply brutalizing to the human spirit." Sebastian Junger, Tribe (New York: Hachette Book Group, 2016), 23.

# 6

# The Warrior's Method of Processing Combat

War overwhelms the senses and touches the recesses of the warrior. It does not leave an individual the same. The impact of David's combat experience echoes this testimony of history, research, and common sense. Though battle worn, David was a steady, resilient, healthy warrior. His commitment to processing his journey contributed significantly to his well-being. The Psalms catalogue David's inner-workings and open a window into how a God-fearing veteran hammers out his experiences.[60] The above has

---

60 "The psalms were used at key moments in telling of the story of David to clarify and sharpen the narrative episode." Nogalski, "Reading David in the Psalter," 168-169. Nogalski notes thirteen psalms that

covered the imprecatory psalms as a mechanism for processing anger and vengeance, to this, David adds psalms of lament, thanksgiving, and praise.[61]

David was as comfortable with pen and lyre as he was with his sword. His battle rhythm was fight and pray, wage war and sing. Worship was his coping mechanism. He emptied his strength on the battlefield and then emptied his soul before God.

At times, celebration and thanksgiving were the posture of his prayers after combat. He discerned the

---

function explicitly in this manner: Psalms 3, 7, 18, 34, 51, 52, 54, 56, 57, 60, 63, 142. Significantly, every one of these thirteen psalms containing Davidic superscriptions have war, combat, and enemies as their primary context. This furthers the argument that the Psalms can and should be read as a warrior's manual. According to Skinner, "The historical superscriptions are also similar to 'historical psalms' in that they allude to events addressed in other parts of the Hebrew Bible explicitly signifying a contextual setting for complementary understandings. For the reader, there is a constant shift between biography and autobiography. Biblical narratives rarely give insights into the internal state of the character other than the narrator's voice. The historical superscriptions alert the reader to the reality of a self-awareness of the Psalmist. The reader is given another view of history with more information akin to a synoptic view." Skinner, "The Historical Superscriptions of Davidic Psalms," 364.

61 Hermann Gunkel, The Psalms: A Form-Critical Introduction (Philadelphia: Fortress Press, 1967), 1-39.

true source of victory and exalted the Divine Warrior in these moments.[62] Sacrifices of gratitude were made, homecoming celebrations were had, and God was glorified. Recognition of God's protection and care in the face of death was met with shouting and joy. This post-war celebration is a wartime discipline that today's military would do well to imitate. Worship follows the same principle of physical exercise: the greater the rigor, the healthier the individual. Fervent worship is a catalyst for warrior wellness.

In the midst of post-war thanksgiving and celebration, grief is never far off. Paul's dictum "sorrowful, yet always rejoicing" (2 Cor 6:10) may capture the emotive complexity of the returning warrior. At times, the

---

62 "Examination of the Psalter as a whole demonstrates that a number of Divine Warrior victory songs are attested. The following songs are listed together as those songs that focus on singing the praises of the Divine Warrior after victory. They are generically similar on the basis of content, setting, motifs and language—Psalms 18, 20, 21, 24, 29, 46, 47, 66, 68, 76, 93, 96, 97, 98, 114, 118, 124, 125, 136. At this point mention should also be made of a few poems outside of the Psalter that are also Divine Warrior victory songs: Numbers 21:27-30; Exodus 15; Judges 5; Habakkuk 3." Tremper Longman III., "Psalm 98: A Divine Warrior Victory Song," Journal of the Evangelical Theological Society 27, no. 3 (1984): 274. See also, Brettler, "Images of YHWH the Warrior in the Psalms," 135-161.

inverse may be more accurate: "rejoicing, yet always sorrowful." David knew this well. He is masterful when navigating the terrain of pain and disillusionment. The lament psalms document these skillful maneuvers while equipping today's combatant to follow in his steps.[63]

Lament psalms, which make up a significant portion of the psalter, are the warrior's invitation to meet God in a place of disorientation.[64] They give voice to agony, trauma, and fear. They ask hard questions, refuse easy

---

63 Stephen Meyer draws out two important functions of the Psalms for the reader/counselee. "First, the symbolic language of the psalm allows for the expression of difficulties and emotions not expressible through normal prosaic language. Second, the depth of expression may allow the troubled person to identify with another human being in comparable difficulty and thus find hope through the other's experience." Stephen G. Meyer, "The Psalms and Personal Counseling," Journal of Psychology and Theology 2, no. 1 (1974), 26. See also, James D. Roecker, "Use of the Davidic Psalms is an Effective Way to Counsel Military Personnel with Post Traumatic Stress Disorder" (MDiv thesis, Wisconsin Luther Seminary, 2015), 1.

64 Brueggemann suggests a "sequence of orientation, disorientation and reorientation as a helpful way to understand the use and function of the psalms." The psalms of disorientation are individual and corporate laments that enable someone to enter "linguistically into a new distressful situation in which the old orientation has collapsed... lament manifests Israel at its best, giving authentic expression to the real experiences of life." Walter Brueggemann, The Psalms & the Life of Faith (Minneapolis: Fortress Press, 1995), 9, 67.

answers, and revolt against quick-fix solutions. Though some have suggested that lament is an act of "unfaith," in reality it is a courageous expression of trust.[65] God calls His people to bring more than joy and thankfulness into His presence; He calls us to bring our pain.[66]

The language of lament gave David speech when facing his enemies, running for his life, experiencing betrayal, processing combat trauma, and voicing moral wounds. While lament served David as an individual, it had communal dimensions as well. David led his army and his civilians in corporate lament over the death

65 "The faith expressed in the lament is nerve—it is a faith that knows that honest facing of distress can be done effectively only in dialogue with God who acts in transforming ways." Brueggemann, The Psalms & the Life of Faith, 69. As Patrick Miller asserts, "The complaint itself is an act of trust." Sally A. Brown and Patrick D. Miller, Lament: Reclaiming Practices in Pulpit, Pew, and Public Square (Louisville: Westminster John Knox Press, 2005), xv.

66 "The biblical community knows about the pain which needs no theoretical justification. It knows it is simply there. It lingers there relentlessly, silently, heavily. Moreover the biblical community knows that pain cannot be handled alone. In isolation, the power of pain grows more ominous and more hurtful. The pain must be handled in community, even if a community of only a few who will attend. It knows that finally pain must be submitted to the power of the Holy God." Walter Brueggemann, Israel's Praise: Doxology against Idolatry and Ideology (Philadelphia, Fortress Press, 1988), 136.

of its warriors.[67] In modeling sorrow over his fallen combatants, he invited others to embrace the healthy principle: when warriors fall, warriors grieve.

Research demonstrates the importance of processing traumatic experiences and the direct link of prayer to well-being.[68] Lament is an essential pathway toward healing for the war-torn vet. Individual and communal lament both function in critical ways, enabling warriors to work out their experiences before God and others.[69]

---

67 Tod Linafelt, "Private Poetry and Public Eloquence in 2 Samuel 1:17–27: Hearing and Overhearing David's Lament for Jonathan and Saul," Journal of Religion 88, no. 4 (2008): 500-501; Yisca Zimran, "'Look the King is Weeping and Mourning!': Expressions of Mourning in the David Narratives and their Interpretive Contribution," Journal for the Study of the Old Testament 41, no. 4 (2018): 491-517; Guy Darshan, "The Reinterment of Saul and Jonathan's bones (2 Sam 21:12-14) in light of Ancient Greek Hero-Cult Stories," Zeitschrift fur die alttestamentliche Wissenschaft 125, no. 4 (2013): 640-645. These articles all point to the importance of honoring the fallen.

68 Rivka Tuval-Mashiach and others, "Coping with Trauma: Narrative and Cognitive Perspectives," Psychiatry Interpersonal & Biological Processes, 67, no. 3 (2004): 280-293: Koenig, "Religion, Spirituality, and Health," 1-15.

69 "If religious communities are to be authentic, they must incorporate lament within their worship services...Biblical lament expressed in corporate worship is uniquely fitted to provide therapeutic benefit for trauma victims...When others join the sufferer, there is 'consensual validation' that the suffering means something. The

In this same vein, there is an abundance of material on grieving well and the negative effects of inhibited grief.[70] Lament provides the blueprint for solid grief

community votes with its tears that there is something worth weeping over." Further Carlson states, "Suffering that cannot be named, cannot be spoken, cannot be told, can neither be healed nor redressed...lament invites trauma victims to interpret traumatic experience through their covenant relationship with God in Jesus Christ, rather than through faulty schemas. Biblical lament does not passively accept traumatic experience (especially interpersonal trauma); it thrusts it toward God with all the strength indignant hurt can muster and cries, 'Why?' Likewise, biblical lament rips the bandages away from the aftermath of traumatic experience, praying that Yahweh will notice, screaming, 'How long O Lord?'" Nathaniel A. Carlson, "Lament: The Biblical Language of Trauma," A Journal for Theology and Culture 11, no. 1 (2015): 62-67. Brueggemann explores the lack of lament in the North American church and how it affects spiritual health. "In the absence of lament, we may be engaged in uncritical history-stifling praise. Both psychological inauthenticity and social immobility may be derived from the loss of these texts. If we care about authenticity and justice, the recovery of these texts is urgent." Walter Brueggemann, "The Costly Loss of Lament," Journal for the Study of the Old Testament 36 (1986): 67. See also, Glen E. Harris, "A Wounded Warrior Looks at Psalm 13," The Journal of Pastoral Theology (2010): 1-2.

70 Carol Ott, "The impact of complicated grief on mental and physical health at various points in the bereavement process," Death Studies 27, no. 3 (2003): 249-272; M. Katerine Shear, "Grief and mourning gone awry: Pathway and course of complicated grief," Dialogues Clin Neurosci, 14, no. 2 (2012): 119-128; Susan Klein, "Good Grief: A Medical Challenge," Trauma, 5, no. 4 (2003): 261-271; Keith Campbell, "NT Lament in Current Research and its Implications for American

work.[71] David provides a pathway to warfighter wellness encapsulated in the psalms.

_____

Evangelicals," The Journal of Evangelical Theological Society 57, no. 4 (2014): 757-772. Campbell provides a thorough review of scholarly research on lament in the New Testament and concludes it is a viable practice for new covenant believers.

71 The book of Lamentations is a biblical guide to grief. Structured as a Hebrew acrostic, it provides the A to Z of mourning. Leslie Allen states that the book is "a liturgy intended as a therapeutic ritual." Leslie C. Allen, A Liturgy of Grief: A Pastoral Commentary on Lamentations (Ada: Baker Academic, 2011), 8.

# 7

# The Warrior's Sin,
# Shame, and Guilt

David's predominance in the Old Testament is indisputable; as the voluminous material about him confirms this fact. But it is more than the number of pages written about David that draws readers to him, it is his humanness.[72] In David, one sees authenticity;

---

72 Brueggemann recognizes David as a "paradigm for humanness." He further asserts, "What is it that makes David so endlessly fascinating to us? I propose to think this way. On the one hand, David is much like us. There is something genuinely human about him, which means that there is a shape to his life that we can count on and identify with. There is also a freedom about him that makes him interesting and not boring... the narrator cuts through all the royal business to see the man, to see him as an ambiguous, contradictory, enmeshed man, driven and inept, with a range of emotional possibilities... David is not 'cleaned up' in the sense that he is innocent, respectable, or puritanical." We connect with this reality because it is true for us as well; "the truth

brokenness, sin, and failure.[73] In other words, he is relatable. The Bible is honest in its portrayal of its heroes. For warriors, David's brokenness and sin is a source of strength and hope.

Throughout the narratives of David, his brokenness is evident in his family relationships. He struggled parenting his children, demonstrated passivity at critical moments, harbored bitterness and refused to forgive (2 Sam 13:1-21, 14:28-31). Marital tension is a common theme in his life as well (2 Sam 6:16-23, 20:3).[74] At times, David deceived, manipulated, and

---

about ourselves and all of life is finally polyvalent, multi-faceted, and layered. How odd it is that the biblical text knows this best!" Walter Brueggemann, David's Truth: In Israel's Imagination and Memory (Minneapolis: Fortress Press, 2002), 6, 10, 36, 38, 114.

73 "The Bible never denies or downplays David's humanity…He is pious and faithful at times but is also capable of heinous crimes. He is a powerful and decisive man, except around his children whom he cannot control." He concludes that his honest portrayal of David's humanity is compelling to us: "Truth be told, these faults of David's attract our attention more than his virtues. We admire the fearless and pious young hero, but we cannot identify with him. The adulterer who gets caught in a cover-up, on the other hand, is one of us. We empathize with the father who is a failure with his own children." Steven L. McKenzie, King David: A Biography (Oxford: University Press, 2000), 2, 154, 189.

74 1 Chronicles 3:1-8 indicates that David had seven wives. With

was compromised by his political motivation (1 Sam 27:10: 2 Sam 11-12, 18:3, 20:16, 23:18).[75]

As a warrior, David knew his moral boundaries and still transgressed them. He disparaged the dead, lashed out in violence, and teetered on taking life for no just cause (1 Sam 17:51, 25:1-44; 2 Sam 4:9-12). Vengeance and resentment lived in his soul. His dying wish was for violence to be exacted on two men, one whom David allegedly forgave and assured freedom from harm (1 Kgs 2:5-9).[76]

---

his wives he had a total of twenty children, nineteen sons and one daughter. Berković traces God's monogamous design in Scripture and discusses the inevitable dysfunction of polygamous relationships. Danijel Berković, "Marriage and Marital Disputes in the Old Testament," Kairos: Evangelical Journal of Theology 12, no. 2 (2018): 177-180.

75 "He was loyal to his friends, but ruthless to his foes. He was a liar, deceiver, and traitor." J.M.P. Smith, "The Character of King David," Journal of Biblical Literature 52, no. 1 (1993): 11.

76 In the end David is weak and vengeful. "On the literary level and perhaps also on the historical level, in the end the powerful King David became an impotent victim—flaccid, senile, and a tool for his replacement." McKenzie, "Who Was King David?" 364. See also, Greg Goswell, "King and Cultus: The Image of David in the Book of Kings," Journal for the Evangelical Study of the Old Testament 5, no. 2 (2017): 169.

The preeminent story of David's fallenness is a combat story (2 Sam 11-12). It entails a deployed warrior—one of David's loyal mighty men—and his deployed spouse (2 Sam 23:39). It centers on a warrior-king who was supposed to be at war alongside his men. Like Adam and Eve before him, David saw something that was not his and took it by force.[77] David the warrior despised his God and rejected His given word in this moment.

The gravity of this act is heightened by grasping that this is the commander of the entire Israelite army. This is the four-star general taking the wife of the enlisted special operator and doing so while this warrior is

---

77 Scholars have long noted thematic links between the fall of Adam and Eve and the fall of David. Particular links identified have been the progression of temptation to sin, the subtlety of sin, beauty and wisdom, despising God's word, creating one's own definition of good and evil, covering up sin, judgment and the movement from life under blessing and life under curse. The semantic linkages include these: saw (ra'ah), good (tôbat), take (läqach) (Gen 3:20; 2 Sam 11:2; Gen 3:6; 2 Sam 11:4). Phillip G. Camp, "David's Fall: Reading 2 Samuel 11-14 in Light of Genesis 2-4," Restoration Quarterly 53, no. 3 (2011): 150-158. James Ackerman traces this Genesis 2-3 theme through the narrative of David's life. James S. Ackerman, "Knowing Good and Evil: A Literary Analysis of the Court History in 2 Samuel 9-20 and 1 Kings 1-2," Journal of Biblical Literature 109, no. 1 (1990): 41-64.

out risking his life.[78] Called home by the commander, Uriah became victim to David's deceit and attempts at covering his tracks. Uriah's honor circumvented every treacherous move of David. Increasingly desperate, the warrior-king plunged his sword deeper into his own conscience as he penned the order for Uriah's life to be taken.

It was David's hand that ended Uriah.[79] Fratricide

78 David is not ignorant about the woman he pursues. He first inquires as to her identity (2 Sam 11:3). The narrative retelling of the information he finds out is damning. Brueggemann states, "Her name is dangerously hyphenated: 'Bathsheba—daughter of Eliam, wife of Uriah the Hittite.' She has no existence of her own but is identified by the men to whom she belongs." Further Brueggemann states, "Uriah will not sleep with his wife while the war continues. How different David, who sleeps with the wife of another man while that man is risking his life for David in a war that was David's war." Brueggemann, Interpretation: 1-2 Samuel, 273, 275.

79 Nathan's condemnation of David's action in 2 Sam 12:9 is broken into five categories: 1) you have despised the word of the Lord; 2) you have done what is evil in God's sight; 3) you have struck down Uriah the Hittite with the sword; 4) you have taken his wife to be your wife; and 5) you have killed Uriah with the sword of the Ammonites. Of note is the double reference to taking Uriah's life. In the first instance it is David holding the sword. In the second, it is David putting the sword into the hand of his enemies to take the life of Uriah. The wickedness of the act is elevated by the unspoken partnership David made with the Ammonites to take Uriah out.

is horrific and damaging enough for all involved; this, however, was a case of first-degree murder. David's violent betrayal rippled out into his troops who obeyed his orders, exposing them to moral injury. His callous response to the execution of his order matched the condition of his heart.[80] He showed no remorse. Without hesitation, he descended further as he wed a grieving spouse.

The Bible is unflinching in its portrayal of David's sin, as he violates the essence of the warrior code. He manipulates, deceives, betrays, and kills the men who loyally obey him. He forcefully violates the vulnerable deployed spouse and robs her of the life for which she

---

80 "Do not let this matter displease you, for the sword devours now one and now another" (2 Sam 11:25) is David's response. "David's cynicism reaches its culmination here, even as the story reaches its culmination. In his fear and anxiety, David has set himself against the whole moral tradition of his people." Brueggemann, Interpretation: 1-2 Samuel, 278-279.

sacrifices.[81] He abuses his authority.[82] He breaks trust with his troops and his nation. His action in today's military would have him stripped of his uniform and sentenced to prison.

It must be emphasized that the fall of David starts with a sin against his vocation.[83] He should have been

81 David definitely used positional force, whether physical force was included is not clear in the text. "On whether David raped Bathsheba or not, we first note that David's lordship of the sexual encounter, which hinges on the power difference between him and Bathsheba, creates an opening for a subtle (non-physical) use of coercion by David, but to conclude that he 'raped' Bathsheba (in the Hebrew biblical understanding of 'rape') would be to push the evidence too far and read too much of our contemporary conception of rape into the biblical text." Alexander Izuchukwu Abasili, "Was it Rape? The David and Bathsheba Pericope Re-examined," Vetus Testamentum 61 (2011): 14.

82 2 Sam 11-12 is a "narrative of David's blatant abuse of power in adultery and murder." Bernard Frank Batto, Kathryn L. Roberts, and J.J.M Roberts, David and Zion: Biblical Studies in Honor of J.J.M. Roberts (University Park: Eisenbrauns, 2004), 98.

83 Smith rightly observes that the image of David "not accompanying all Israel to war at this time but remaining in Jerusalem may well reflect the narrator's criticism of David as having neglected one of his traditional royal duties." Richard G. Smith, The Fate of Justice and Righteousness During David's Reign: Narrative Ethics and Rereading the Court History According to 2 Samuel 8:15-20:26 (New York: T&P Clark, 2009), 121.

shoulder to shoulder with Uriah. He should have been wearing his uniform, not sitting on his roof. This fatal move has a domino effect. The narrative unfolds the movement described by one New Testament author: "Each person is tempted when he is lured and enticed by his own desire. Then desire when it has conceived gives birth to sin, and sin when it is fully grown brings forth death" (James 1:14-15). David's action forever changed his life.[84]

This section started with the assertion that David's brokenness brings hope to the warrior. How can that be? An honest look in the mirror requires embracing the fact that David's actions are not beyond any of us. If warriors cannot see themselves in David and David in themselves, then they do not know themselves.[85] The

---

84 Forgiveness is immediate while the consequences for David's actions linger. God's discipline will never cease: "The sword shall never depart from your house" (2 Sam 12:10). Uriah is a permanent blot on David's record (1 Kgs 15:5) and Bathsheba will forever be the wife of Uriah, not David (2 Sam 12:15; Matt 1:6). Brueggemann, Interpretation: 1-2 Samuel, 281.

85 Brueggemann argues that if we honestly face this text we are forced to "face the harder questions of human desire and human power—desire with all its delight, power with all its potential for death...the writer has cut very, very deep into the strange web of foolishness, fear and fidelity that comprises the human map. The narrative is more than

raw portrayal of David communicates that a man of God and a man of war is also a broken, frail, struggling human being. This painful reality is also a hope-filled one.

David is not left hopeless in his hopelessness. The narrative reveals a gracious God that pursues this warrior with discipline and mercy. God sent a prophet to confront David, conveying that He had not left this man of God to his own devices. When the gravity of his actions landed on him, David owned it.[86] He made no excuse, but confessed: "I have sinned." His three-word confession expands when he picks up the pen to write one of the greatest psalms.

Psalm 51 is a penitent's guide for the morally

we want to know about David and more than we want to understand about ourselves." Brueggemann, Interpretation: 1-2 Samuel, 272.

86 "There is not much to celebrate about David in this narrative. The narrator nevertheless wants us to notice two things about this portrayal of David. First, concerning David, it is evident that David still has a considerable degree of moral courage and sensitivity. He is able to face up to his real situation. Second, concerning the gospel, though it is late in the narrative, it is not too late for David's repentance. David is a man who is still willing and able to cast himself on Yahweh's mercy." Brueggemann, Interpretation: 1-2 Samuel, 282.

compromised warrior.[87] This psalm catalogues David's ownership over the external and internal, vertical and horizontal, individual and communal, dimensions of his transgressions.[88] His confession is relentless and thorough as he links his conception in sin to the Bathsheba debacle and refuses to shift blame for his actions. His petitions are bold and unwavering as he asks for mercy, forgiveness, restoration, cleansing, a clean heart, a right spirit, the presence of God, joy, and an open mouth to praise. His trust in God's covenant loyalty is unshakable as he leans into the mercy of God, the saving passion of the Lord, and the posture

---

87 Frederick Gaiser argues that Psalm 50 functions as a call to repentance while Psalm 51 encapsulates the way of repentance. Frederick J. Gaiser, "The David of Psalm 51: Reading Psalm 51 in Light of Psalm 50," Word & World 23, no. 4 (2003): 382. See also, David A. Covington, "Psalm 51: Repenter's Guide," The Journal of Biblical Counseling 20, no.1 (2001): 21-39.

88 "Psalm 51 looks like a 'V,' tracking the movement of David's Holy-Spirit-guided look at his past, present, and future. The 'V' traces the descent of David's attention, graphed as it were along a time-line from left to right. David's prayer attention moves from the outer world of his sins downward to the inner world of his heart, then on and down to the exchange of sin for righteousness in blood sacrifice; from there on and up to David's new heart, and then up again to the outer world of action and society." Covington, "Psalm 51: Repenter's Guide," 23.

of the Holy God toward contrition.[89]

How does God respond to David's extreme ownership? Through the mouth of Nathan, the confronting prophet, he speaks: "The Lord also has put away your sin, you shall not die" (2 Sam 12:13). Total forgiveness is God's gracious response to his layered sin. Warriors may ask: Can God ever forgive me for the heinous things I have seen, done, or failed to do?[90] David's story gives the answer. The answer is

[89] "Psalm 51 (vv. 3-11) begins with an appeal to God's mercy (or grace), merciful love (more literally, covenant loyalty or 'esed), and abundant compassion, three attributes that are part of the foundational description of God in Exodus 34:6." Peter Nasuti, "Repentance and Transformation: The Role of the Spirit in Psalm 51," The Bible Today 57, no. 4 (2019): 215.

[90] In this one narrative, the sin committed and forgiven includes failing to fulfill one's military duty, lusting after another man's wife, researching a forbidden wife's identity and proceeding with the sinful desire, forceful adultery with a deployed spouse, lying and manipulating to cover up the adultery, deceiving and tricking the victim's husband, conspiring to murder a fellow-uniform wearer, pulling other soldiers into the web of deception, killing the warrior with a military order, viewing the lives of other men as collateral damage to cloaking one's evil, taking the lives of other innocent soldiers while killing one innocent soldier, giving a soldier into the hands of the enemy to be killed, being callous and nonchalant about causing the deaths of loyal soldiers, taking the fallen soldier's wife and marrying her, grossly misusing power and authority, rejecting and despising God's clear word on leading and caring for warriors, betraying

hope for the warrior.

David, like Paul, sees himself as the chief of sinners. He recognizes that even his moral failure is useful for pointing others to the mercy of God. Paul's language could just as well be David's: "Christ Jesus came into the world to save sinners, of whom I am the foremost. But I received mercy for this reason, that in me, as the foremost, Jesus Christ might display his perfect patience as an example to those who were to believe in him for eternal life" (1 Tim 1:15-16). This is pure hope for the warfighter.[91]

---

the biblical warrior's code, being driven by selfishness, being controlled by pride, and rejecting God himself. David's words are potent: "If you, O Lord, should mark iniquities who could stand? But with you there is forgiveness that you may be feared" (Ps 130:3-4). A.A. Anderson, Word Biblical Commentary: 2 Samuel (Dallas: Word Books Publisher, 1989), 156.

91 Stanley Walters explores how David's words can and should become our words. When his confession becomes ours, so does his hope. Stanley D. Walters, "I talk of my sin (to God) (and to you): Psalm 51, with David speaking," Calvin Theological Journal 50, no. 1 (2015): 91-109.

8

# The Warrior's Gospel Dependence

The final mark of the man of God and the man of war is gospel reliance. The discussion of the warrior's sin, shame, and guilt leads nicely to this point. The profession of arms is freighted with moral challenges. Living and moving in a high-stakes vocation requires anchoring. A number of critical anchor points for the warrior have been covered. The gospel is another integral anchor point, as it forms the foundational hope for forgiveness, reconciliation, redemption, and hope.

The narrative architecture of the David story is centered on Jesus.[92] It leans forward to the coming of

_____

92 James M. Hamilton Jr., "The Typology of David's Rise to Power: Messianic Pattern in the Book of Samuel," The Southern Baptist Journal

another David, a greater one (Matt 1:1, 21:9; Rom 1:3). David himself recognized this dimension of his own storyline (Psalm 16, 22).[93] David's hope was ultimately a gospel hope. He anticipated the coming Christ.[94] As a prophet, he spoke of the day when the covenant God made with him would climax in the incarnation, death, and resurrection of the Son of God (Acts 1:16, 2:25-36, 4:25, 13:33-37).[95]

David's prototypical faith in the cross and empty tomb was a justifying trust (Rom 4:6-8).[96] He knew God the Warrior, and trusted him in battle and in life. In faith, he anticipated the day when this God would

---

of Theology 16, no. 2 (2012): 4-18; Don Collett, "The Christology of Israel's Psalter," Currents in Theology and Mission 4, no. 6 (2014): 390-395.

93 Jouette M. Bassler, "A Man for All Seasons: David in Rabbinic and New Testament Literature." Interpretation 40, no. 2 (1986): 164.

94 Christopher G. Norden, "Paul's Use of the Psalms in Romans: A Critical Analysis," Evangelical Quarterly 88, no. 1 (2016): 71-88.

95 Ibid, 168; Peter Doble, "Luke 24:26, 44—Songs of God's Servant: David and his Psalms in Luke-Acts," Journal for the Study of the New Testament 28, no. 3 (2006): 281.

96 Jackson Wu, "Why Is God Justified in Romans? Vindicating Paul's Use of Psalm 51 in Romans 3:4," Neotestamentica 51, no. 2 (2017): 310. Wu argues that Paul "presents David as a paradigm of one who is justified apart from the law."

armor up with human flesh (Ps 40:6; Heb 10:5). In the deployed Son, we behold the intersection of God the warrior and God the human being. As such, he is both the rescuer of the warfighter (Acts 10:1, 47-48) and the ultimate expression of a warrior (Col 2:13-15; Heb 2:14-15; Rev 19:11-16).

With the cross as his weapon, Jesus fights for sinful David. The suspended wrath earned by David's sin is placed upon Christ the substitute (Rom 3:21-26). David's sins committed on the battlefield, in the bedroom, among his family, and elsewhere are covered by Jesus (Rom 4:4-8). Forgiveness, cleansing, and wholeness are secured when the tomb is vacated on the third day. The gospel is good news for the heavy-hearted vet.

The gospel does not patronize the agony of the warrior's burden; instead, it affirms the soul-wrenching impact of war. It points to the anguish of Golgotha: to a fierce, sweating, bleeding, dying warrior who has taken into himself the horrors of our actions. That hill outside Jerusalem was an unforgiving war zone. In that place, the Son of God, the man of sorrows, expressed profound solidarity with war torn humanity.

Nor does the gospel let men off the hook for their actions. The death of Christ is a commentary on the gravity of our wrongdoing, a fierce condemnation of sin. Accountability is central to that dark moment. This is an important dimension of the gospel for the man who knows that judgment is deserved. Ironically, hope is located where sin is condemned.

In Christ sin is judged and settled before the just judge of the universe. The cold lifeless tomb is where the record of our every wrong is buried. The resurrected Christ guarantees that sin, death, and Satan are undone. The gospel speaks to a righteousness apart from the actions or merits of humanity (Rom 3:28). It is the good news of transfer: man's wrongdoing for Christ's right doing (2 Cor 5:21).

The person and work of Christ anchors the soul and steadies the heart against the onslaught of regret and shame (Heb 6:19; Eph 6:16; Rom 10:11). It arms the warrior for a different battle (Eph 6:11). The gospel yells "no condemnation" over the nagging voice of guilt (Rom 8:1). It is a healing balm to a seared conscience (Heb 9:14, 10:22; 1 Pet 3:21). It is a clean slate that covers over the past (1 Jn 1:9). The gospel is dogged hope for the well-adjusted and wounded warrior (Col 1:23).

# A Final Word to the Warrior

David is the blueprint of the godly soldier. His life models the intersection of the warrior vocation and the life of faith. The narrative window into David's life is a treasure trove for those facing similar challenges today. David provides an example of how the treacherous terrain of soldiering is navigated before the face of God. In him, the biblical marks of warrior health are discernible: gospel dependence, a life of repentance, embrace of lament, a leaning heavily on community, a right posture toward enemies, a theological grasp of war, a solid relationship with God, and a steady diet of God's Word.

The stories of David and the psalms teach the warfighter that guidance and grounding flow from the Word of God, freedom and expression come through prayer and song, solidarity and support is provided by community, and redemption and hope are found in the Divine Warrior who comes in the flesh. The literature on David touches moral complexities in the profession of arms, including proper posture toward enemies, the function of the image of God in warfighting, the role of the conscience, moral injury, honoring the fallen, the temptations unique to warriors, relational strain on families, the power of shame and guilt, and the role of forgiveness.

David's story is rugged; its authenticity is intrinsically life-giving for the contemporary combatant. His journey confirms that living and operating in the kill chain leaves no one untouched. 1-2 Samuel is an exposé of the impact of living in death's shadow. Yet, the raw narrative is equally infused with faith and health. The realism of his story speaks hope to today's military member and equips them to navigate with skill and strength.

# APPENDIX

# The S.T.R.O.N.G. Model

The S.T.R.O.N.G. framework is an attempt to operationalize the principles of warrior health discerned in David's journey. They encapsulate the model of faith for the warfighter that has been proposed throughout the book.

# STRONG

| STUDY | TRAIN | RELY | OFFER | NAME | GRASP |
|---|---|---|---|---|---|
| the sacred text | the conscience | on community | prayer & song | sin & guilt | mercy & hope |
| The study of the Word of God equips a warrior with the right view of God, self and the world. It provides the warrior with a moral code and perspective on all matters pertaining to the warfighting vocation. | The biblical warrior code grounds and protects an individual when properly applied. The conscience must first be educated and then trained for the warrior to operate adeptly in a combat environment. | The community plays a key role in stabilizing the warfighter. The practice of solidarity, the provision of combat rituals, the creation of a safe context for confession and the role of communal worship all ensure health. | Processing the full scope of emotion and experience is essential for warrior health. The practice of prayer and song provided in the Psalms gives voice to the warrior's layered emotions and experiences. | The need for confession and repentance is utmost in warrior health. Refusing to hide, naming one's actions and taking full responsibility for them moves an individual to forgiveness, health and peace. | Warriors carry heavy loads, a place and invitation to unload is necessary. The gospel promise of mercy, forgiveness and certain hope is fuel for the warfighter's journey and assurance of wellbeing. |

# BIBLIOGRAPHY

Adsit, Chris. *The Combat Trauma Healing Manual: Christ-centered Solutions for Combat Trauma.* Newport News: Military Ministry Press, 2007.

Anderson, Gary A. "King David and the Psalms of Imprecation." *Pro Ecclesia* 15, no. 3 (2006).

Anderson, G.W. "Enemies and evildoers in the Book of Psalms." *Bulletin of the John Rylands Library* 48, no. 1 (1965).

Athas, George. "'A Man after God's Own Heart': David and the Rhetoric of Election to Kingship." *Journal for the Evangelical Study of the Old Testament* 2, no. 2 (2013).

Bailey, Kenneth. *The Good Shepherd: A Thousand Year Journey from Psalm 23 to the New Testament.* Downers Grove: IVP Academic, 2014.

Ballard Jr., H. Wayne. "Reading the Psalms in Light of 9-11: The Dialectic of War and Peace as Leitmotif in the Psalms of Ascents." *Perspectives in Religious Studies* 31, no. 4 (2004).

Bang, Jeung-Yeoul. "The Canonical Function of Psalms 19 and 119 as Macro-Torah Frame." *The Korean Journal of Old Testament Studies* 66 (2017).

Barshinger, David P. "Spite or Spirit? Jonathan Edwards on the Imprecatory Language of the Psalms." *Westminster Theological Journal* 77 (2015).

Bassler, Jouette M. "A Man for All Seasons: David in Rabbinic and New Testament Literature." *Interpretation* 40, no. 2 (1986).

Bosworth, David. A. "Faith and Resilience: King David's Reaction to the Death of Bathsheba's Firstborn." *The Catholic Biblical Quarterly* 73 (2011).

———. "Evaluating King David: Old Problems and Recent Scholarship." *The Catholic Biblical Quarterly* 68, no. 2 (2006).

Brettler, Marc. "Images of YHWH the Warrior in the Psalms." *Semeia* 61 (1993).

Brueggemann, Walter. "The Costly Loss of Lament." *Journal for the Study of the Old Testament* 36 (1986).

_____. *David's Truth: In Israel's Imagination and Memory.* Minneapolis: Fortress Press, 2002.

_____. *Interpretation, A Biblical Commentary for Teaching and Preaching: First and Second Samuel.* Louisville: John Knox Press, 1990.

_____. *Israel's Praise: Doxology against Idolatry and Ideology.* Philadelphia, Fortress Press, 1988.

_____. *The Message of the Psalms: A Theological Commentary.* Minneapolis: Fortress Press, 1985.

_____. *The Psalms & the Life of Faith.* Minneapolis: Fortress Press, 1995.

Bruneau, Emile, and Nour Kteily. "The enemy as animal: Symmetric dehumanization during asymmetric warfare." *Plos One* 12, no. 7 (2017).

Carlson, Nathaniel A. "Lament: The Biblical Language of Trauma." *A Journal for Theology and Culture* 11, no. 1 (2015).

Carson, D.A. *The Difficult Doctrine of the Love of God.* Wheaton, IL: Crossway Books, 2000.

Chisholm Jr., Robert B. "Yahweh's Self Revelation in Deed and Word: A Biblical Theology of 1-2 Samuel." *Southwestern Journal of Theology* 55, no. 2 (2013).

Colijn, Brenda B. *Images of Salvation in the New Testament.* Downers Grove: IVP Academic, 2010.

Collett, Don. "The Christology of Israel's Psalter." *Currents in Theology and Mission* 41, no. 6 (2014).

Coppenger, Mark. "The Golden Rule and War." *Criswell Theological Review* 4, no. 2 (1990).

Corey, David Dwyer. "Luther and the Just-War Tradition." *Political Theology* 12, no. 2 (2011).

Craigie, Peter C. *Word Biblical Commentary: Psalms 1-50.* Waco: Word Books Publisher, 1983.

Creach, Jerome F.D., *Yahweh as Refuge and the Editing of the Hebrew Psalter.* Sheffield, UK: Sheffield Academic Press, 1996.

Daly-Denton, Margaret. "David the Psalmist, Inspired Prophet: Jewish Antecedents of a New Testament Datum." *Australian Biblical Review* 52 (2004).

Darshan, Guy. "The Reinterment of Saul and Jonathan's bones (2 Sam 21:12-14) in light of Ancient Greek Hero-Cult Stories." *Zeitschrift fur die alttestamentliche Wissenschaft* 125, no. 4 (2013).

Day, John N. "The Imprecatory Psalms and Christian Ethics." *Bibliotheca Sacra* 159 (2002).

DeClaisse-Walford, Nancy L. *The Shape and Shaping of the Book of Psalms: The Current State of Scholarship.* Atlanta: SBL Press, 2014.

DeRouchie, Jason S. "The Heart of YHWH and His Chosen One in 1 Samuel 13:14." *Bulletin for Biblical Research* 24, no. 4 (2014).

Fraser, James H. "The Authenticity of the Psalm Titles." ThM diss., Grace Theological Seminary, 1984.

French, Susan E. *The Code of the Warrior: Exploring Warrior Values Past and Present.* New York: Rowman & Littlefield Publishers, 2003.

_____. "The Code of the Warrior: Ideals of Warrior Cultures Throughout History." *The Journal of Character & Leadership Integration* (2017).

_____. "Dehumanizing the Enemy: The Intersection of Neuroethics and Military Ethics." In *Responsibilities to Protect: Perspectives in Theory and Practice,* edited by David Whetham and Bradley J. Strawser. Boston: Brill Nijhoff, 2015.

Frisch, Amos. "Comparison with David as a Means of Evaluating Character in the Book of Kings." *The Journal of Hebrew Scriptures* 11, no. 4 (2011).

Gard, Daniel L., "The Chronicler's David: Saint and Sinner." *Concordia Theological Quarterly* 70 (2006).

Garsiel, Moshe. "David's Elite Warriors and their Exploits in the Books of Samuel and Chronicles." *The Journal of Hebrew Scriptures* 11 (2011).

Gerstenberger, Erhard S. "Enemies and Evildoers in the Psalms: A Challenge to Christian Preaching." *Horizons in Biblical Theology* 4, no. 5 (1983).

Goswell, Greg. "King and Cultus: The Image of David in the Book of Kings." *Journal for the Evangelical Study of the Old Testament* 5, no. 2 (2017).

Grimell, Jan. "Contemporary Insights from Biblical Combat Veterans through the Lenses of Moral Injury and Post-Traumatic Stress Disorder." *Journal of Pastoral Care & Counseling* 72, no. 4 (2018).

Grossman, David. *On Killing: The Psychological Costs of Learning to Kill in War and Society.* New York: Back Bay Books, 2009.

Hamilton, James. "The Typology of David's Rise to Power: Messianic Pattern in the Book of Samuel." *The Southern Baptist Journal of Theology* 16, no. 2 (2012).

Hamlin-Glover, Denise L. "Spirituality, Religion, and Resilience Among Military Families." PhD diss., Florida State University, 2009.

Hankle, Dominic D. "The Therapeutic Implications of the Imprecatory Psalms in the Christian Counseling Setting." *Journal of Psychology and Theology* 38, no. 4 (2010).

Harris, Glenn E. "A Wounded Warrior Looks at Psalm 13." *The Journal of Pastoral Theology* (2010).

Herman, Judith. *Trauma and Recovery: The Aftermath of Violence—from Domestic Abuse to Political Terror.* New York: Basic Books, 1997.

Johnson, Vivian L. *David in Distress: His Portrait through the Historical Psalms.* Edinburgh, UK: T&T Clark, 2009.

Johnston, Laurie. "'Love Your Enemies' Even in the Age of Terrorism." *Political Theology* 6, no. 1 (2005).

Junger, Sebastian. *Tribe.* New York: Hachette Book Group, 2016.

Kaiser Jr., Walter C. "The Structure of the Book of Psalms." *Bibliotheca Sacra* 174 (2017).

Kirk, Alan. "'Love your enemies' the Golden Rule, and ancient reciprocity (Luke 6:27-35)." *Journal of Biblical Literature* 122, no. 4 (2003).

Klein, Ralph W. "David: Sinner and Saint in Samuel and Chronicles." *Currents in Theology and Mission* 26, no. 2 (1999).

_____. *Word Biblical Commentary: 1 Samuel.* Waco: Word Books Publisher, 1983.

Knoppers, Gary. "Images of David in Early Judaism: David as Repentant Sinner in Chronicles." *Biblica* 76, no. 4 (1995).

Kuruvilla, Abraham. "David v. Goliath (1 Samuel 17): What is the Author Doing with what He is saying?" *Journal of the Evangelical Theological Society* 58, no. 3 (2015).

Larson, Duane, and Jeff Zust. *Care for the Sorrowing Soul: Healing Moral Injuries from Military Service and Implications for the Rest of Us.* Eugene: Cascade Books, 2017.

Linafelt, Tod. "Private Poetry and Public Eloquence in 2 Samuel 1:17–27: Hearing and Overhearing David's Lament for Jonathan and Saul." *Journal of Religion* 88, no. 4 (2008).

Linafelt, Tod, Timothy Beal, and Claudia V. Camp. *The Fate of King David: The Past and Present of a Biblical Icon.* Edinburgh, UK: T&T Clark, 2010.

Longman III, Tremper. *How to Read the Psalms.* Downers Grove: InterVarsity Press, 1988.

_____. "Psalm 98: A Divine Warrior Victory Song." *Journal of the Evangelical Theological Society* 27, no. 3 (1984).

Luther, Martin. *Christians Can Be Soldiers.* Minneapolis: Lutheran Press, 2010.

_____. *Luther's Little* Instruction Book: The *Small Catechism* of Martin *Luther.* Boulder, CO: Project Gutenberg, 1994.

Lyke, Larry L. *King David with the Wise Woman of Tekoa: The Resonance of Tradition in Parabolic Narrative.* Sheffield, UK: Sheffield Academic, 1997.

Mays, James Luther. "The David of the Psalms." *Interpretation* 40 (1986).

Mazar, B. "The Military Elite of King David." *Vetus Testamentum* 13, no. 3 (1963).

McFall, Leslie. "The Chronology of Saul and David." *Journal of the Evangelical Theological Society* 53, no. 3 (2010).

McKenzie, Steven L. *King David: A Biography.* Oxford: University Press, 2000.

_____. "Who Was King David?" *Word & World* 23, no. 4 (2003).

Meyer, Stephen G. "The Psalms and Personal Counseling." *Journal of Psychology and Theology* 2, no. 1 (1974).

Murray, Donald M. "Under YHWH's Veto: David as Shedder of Blood in Chronicles." *Biblica* 82, no. 4 (2001).

Rendon, Jim. *Upside: The New Science of Post-Traumatic Growth*. New York: Touchstone, 2015.

Reynolds, Kent Aaron. *Torah as Teacher: The Exemplary Torah Student in Psalm 119*. Boston: Brill, 2010.

Roecker, James D. "Use of the Davidic Psalms is an Effective Way to Counsel Military Personnel with Post Traumatic Stress Disorder." MDiv thesis, Wisconsin Lutheran Seminary, 2015.

Ruzer, Serge. "'Love Your Enemy' Precept in the Sermon on the Mount in the Context of Early Jewish Exegesis: A New Perspective." *Revue Biblique* 111, no. 2 (2004).

Shay, Jonathan. *Odysseus in America: Combat Trauma and the Trials of Homecoming*. New York: Scribner, 2002.

_____. *Achilles in Vietnam: Combat Trauma and the Undoing of Character*. New York: Scribner, 1994.

Shinan, Avigdor. "King David of the Sages." *Nordisk Judaistik* 24, no. 1 (2003).

Sites, Kevin. *The Things They Cannot Say*. New York: Harper Perennial, 2013.

Skinner, Christopher. "'The Good Shepherd Lays Down His Life for the Sheep' (John 10:11, 15, 17): Questioning the Limits of the Johannine Metaphor." *The Catholic Biblical Quarterly* 80 (2018).

Skinner, Jerome L. "The Historical Superscriptions of Davidic Psalms: An Exegetical, Intertextual, and Methodological Analysis." PhD diss., Andrews University, 2016.

Slabbert, Martin J. "Coping in a harsh reality: The concept of the 'enemy' in the composition of Psalms 9 and 10." *HTS Theological Studies* 71, no. 3 (2015).

Smith, J.M.P. "The Character of King David." *Journal of Biblical Literature* 52, no. 1 (1993).

Steussy, Marti J. "The Enemy in the Psalms." *Word & World* 28, no. 1 (2008).

Stroud, Robert C. "Demonizing Our Enemies & Dehumanizing Ourselves." *Curtana Sword of Mercy* 54 (2009).

Tate, Marvin E. "An Exposition of Psalm 8." *Perspectives in Religious Studies* 28, no. 4 (2001).

Tick, Edward. *Warrior's Return: Restoring the Soul after War.* Boulder: Sounds True, 2014.

Tull, Patricia K. "Jonathan's Gift of Friendship." *Interpretation* 58, no. 2 (2004).

Walters, Stanley D. "I talk of my sin (to God) (and to you): Psalm 51, with David speaking." *Calvin Theological Journal* 50, no. 1 (2015).

Ward, Martin J. "Psalm 109: David's Poem of Vengeance." *Andrews University Seminary Studies* 28, no. 2 (1980).

Whybray, Norman. *Reading the Psalms as a Book.* Sheffield, UK: Sheffield Academic Press, 1996.

Wilson, Stephen M. "Blood Vengeance and the Imago Dei in the Flood Narrative (Genesis 9:6)." *Interpretation: A Journal of Bible and Theology* 71, no. 3 (2017).

Wood, John. *Perspectives on War in the Bible.* Macon, GA: Mercer University Press, 1998.

Yoon, Dong-Young. "The Role of Prophets Gad and Nathan in the Davidic Court." *Korean Journal of Christian Studies* 109 (2018).

Zimran, Yisca. "'Look the King is Weeping and Mourning!': Expressions of Mourning in the David Narratives and their Interpretive Contribution." *Journal for the Study of the Old Testament* 41, no. 4 (2018)

Printed in the USA
CPSIA information can be obtained
at www.ICGtesting.com
LVHW030429090823
754674LV00018B/310

9 781088 080559